Financial Functions With A Spreadsheet

Janet Swift

I/O Press
I Programmer Library

Financial Functions With A Spreadsheet
Copyright © 2016 by Janet Swift

First Edition
First Printing, 2016
Revision 0

Published by IO Press Ltd   www.iopress.info
In association with I Programmer   www.i-programmer.info

ISBN Paperback: 978-1871962017

Preface

Spreadsheets take away the need to be good with arithmetic because they will do the sums for us - no matter how complicated or extended, and never get the wrong answer. This allows us to concentrate on the way that the calculations work rather than the petty arithmetic that they lead to.

Spreadsheets take the hard work out of calculations, but you still need to know how to do them. Before turning our attention to more complex financial formulas, Chapter 1 starts with something that while very familiar can be very confusing – percentages. Then we move on to explore the idea of borrowing money for a specified rate of interest or earning interest on an investment in Chapter 2 and follow this up with the idea of the `effective' interest rate and introduce the much quoted APR, Annual Percentage Rate.

Understanding the way interest rates affect cashflow is the key to both savings and loans. Chapter 4 explores the relationship between Present Value and Future Value with respect to savings plans, Chapter 5 extends this to annuities and Chapter 6 looks at repayment loans. The principles of present and future value apply even if the cashflow is irregular. Chapter 7 introduces formulas for Net Present Value and Net Future Value pointing this is just a matter of breaking down the cashflow calculations into simple steps. In Chapter 8 we explore how these functions can be used to make investment decisions and in Chapter 9 we meet two other key functions for gauging the worth of an investment with an irregular cashflow, the Internal Rate of Return (IRR) and the Modified Internal Rate of Return (MIRR).

Throughout the book sample spreadsheets are presented with details of how you can construct them for yourself and use them for you own investigations and investment decisions. It is assumed that you are already familiar with the basics of using a spreadsheet in general.

Table of Contents

Chapter 1

Understanding Percentages

Many financial calculations make use of the concept of 'per cent', as an interest or tax rate. You almost certainly know what a percentage is, and indeed have known since school days. Yet, however familiar you are with this concept, percentages present many pitfalls that need to be avoided.

So before we move on to exploring the financial functions that spreadsheets make available, let's make sure we have a solid understanding of how percentages work.

So you think you know the percentages?

Before you turn to the next chapter, having decided that there is nothing new here, try the following simple problems.

Don't actually try to work them out, after all that's what a spreadsheet is for, just try to convince yourself that you could, or could not, work them out.

- If you know that the cost is $75 including a 10% discount, what is the undiscounted selling price?

- If you pay tax at a rate of 25% and there is tax relief on a loan subject to interest at 15%, what is the effective interest rate?

- If a salesman offers you a 5% additional discount on a price that is already subject to a 10% discount, what is the total discount?

- If sales tax is 5% and the tax inclusive price is $125, what is the selling price before tax?

Even if you can solve these problems without any difficulty, are you sure you know exactly how you solved them?

One of the difficulties is that we become accustomed to manipulating percentages without being entirely sure of the rationale behind what we are doing.

This is fine until someone challenges you to demonstrate that the result you have reached is indeed fair and reasonable!

Spreadsheets make it easy

Percentage calculations are easy and there is never any need to be in doubt as to why or how they work. Spreadsheets take away the need to be good with arithmetic because they will do the sums for us, no matter how complicated or extended, and never get the wrong answer. This allows us to concentrate on the way that the calculations work rather than the petty arithmetic that they lead to.

Throughout this book we will present ways of thinking about financial calculations that make it easy for you to understand what is happening. These ways are not always the best and most efficient in actually calculating a numerical result but this seldom matters.

Before spreadsheets it was often necessary to find simple, and sometimes approximate, ways of calculating a result. If it had to be done using a calculator or worse, in the head, then it had to be efficient rather than perfectly accurate or, of even less importance - understandable.

You will not find any such tricks or approximations in this book because understanding comes top of the list of priorities.

Why, you may ask, is understanding financial calculations so important?

The answer is that only by understanding the basis for financial calculations can you have any hope of interpreting the results that they produce. Only by understanding can you hope to discover new ideas and new ways of doing things. Understanding is always, and in this case literally, worth something!

The only disadvantage of this approach is that you may find it difficult to see how some of the more ad-hoc methods that you might have been taught fit in. In most cases it is better to forget ad-hoc methods for the moment. In time you will most probably see how they derive from the more direct approach or you will simply forget about them!

Notice that it is assumed that you know how to use a spreadsheet - Excel, Google Sheets or LibreOffice Calc say. The financial functions described in this book work on most spreadsheets perhaps with minor and trivial differences.

Simple percentages

A percentage is simply a fraction expressed as the relevant proportion of 100.

For example, 1/2 or 0.5 is 50% because 50 is half of 100. The fraction and its corresponding percentage are simply two different ways of talking about the same thing and in general we are more familiar with dealing with percentages than the underlying fractions.

For example, a discount of 10% always sounds friendlier than a discount of 0.1.

When it comes to working with spreadsheets however there are many advantages to the fractional form of a percentage. The reason is that while most spreadsheets understand percentages and allow you to enter and use them directly it is only when you enter the fractional form of the percentage can you be 100% (or should that be 1) sure that you are doing the right sum.

For example, to find 50% of the contents of cell A1 you can simply type:

```
=50%*A1
```

but it is important to realize that this is the same as:

```
=A1*50/100
```

or:

```
=A1*0.5
```

This situation is rather worse when it comes to storing percentages in cells and then using them in other calculations.

For example, if B1 contains a percentage, for example 50, then the formula to find that percentage of A1 is:

```
=A1*B1/100
```

The danger here is that, while the B1 seems essential to the calculation, the 100 will soon be forgotten!

Leaving out the necessary factors of 100 is a common error in percentage calculations, but one that is usually quickly spotted and corrected due to the size of the result.

A more important reason for preferring to work with percentages as fractions is that it makes formulas look simpler by eliminating the need to divide every percentage by 100.

Also, we will see in the next section, spreadsheets actually work better with fractions even when they appear to be working with percentages.

Spreadsheets and percentages

The fact that it is easier to work with fractions and easier to interpret percentages causes no problem to a spreadsheet user.

The reason is that nearly all spreadsheets allow you to enter a fraction and display it as a percentage. That is, if you format a cell or range to display as percentages, entering a fraction such as 0.5 will result in 50% being displayed.

This can be the cause of confusion if you are not aware of what is happening.

To make what you enter the same as what is displayed, most spreadsheets will also allow you to enter a percentage using a percent sign.

For example, if you enter 75% then 0.75 is stored in the cell but, as long as a percentage format applies, it will display as 75%. In this case it really is possible to forget what is stored in a cell. The danger is that you will make the mistake of including 100 in all formulas that make use of the apparent percentages. Notice that if you don't set a percentage format then in nearly all cases a percentage will display as a decimal fraction.

	A	B	C	D	E	F	G
1	0.5	<- Entered as 50% but formatted to show as decimal					
2	50%	<- Entered as 50% but formatted to show as percentage					
3							
4	6.17	<- 12.34*A1 is correct					
5	6.17	<- 12.34*A2 is correct					
6	0.0617	<- 12.34*A2/100 is incorrect					
7							

Formatting avoids errors

In the figure above you can see a percentage entered with and without being formatted as a percentage. When trying to work out 50% of the value 12.34 you can see that the temptation is to enter =12.34*A2/100 because A2 looks like a percentage.

Of course it isn't a percentage and so the correct calculation is just

`=12.34*A2`.

That is:

- Always enter a percentage value with a trailing percentage sign

- Always format cells that contain percentages to show as percentages

- Always calculate using percentages as if they were decimal fractions

In the remainder of this book we will use the convention that in all formulas percentages are treated as decimal fractions, for example 90% as 0.9 and 5% as 0.05.

Percentage increase/decrease

Working out a simple percentage should cause no one any difficulties given a spreadsheet or even a pocket calculator.

What is slightly more difficult is to work out is the result of increasing or decreasing a value by a given percentage is.

As long as you think about it in the right way even this isn't difficult. If a value increases by I% then you have the original value plus I% of it where I% is written as a decimal fraction:

```
value + value *I
```

or more simply:

```
value*(1 + I)
```

The quantity $(1 + I)$ occurs so often in financial functions that it is worth remembering it as what you multiply to increase a given value by I%. In the same way to decrease a given value by I% you multiply by $(1 - I)$.

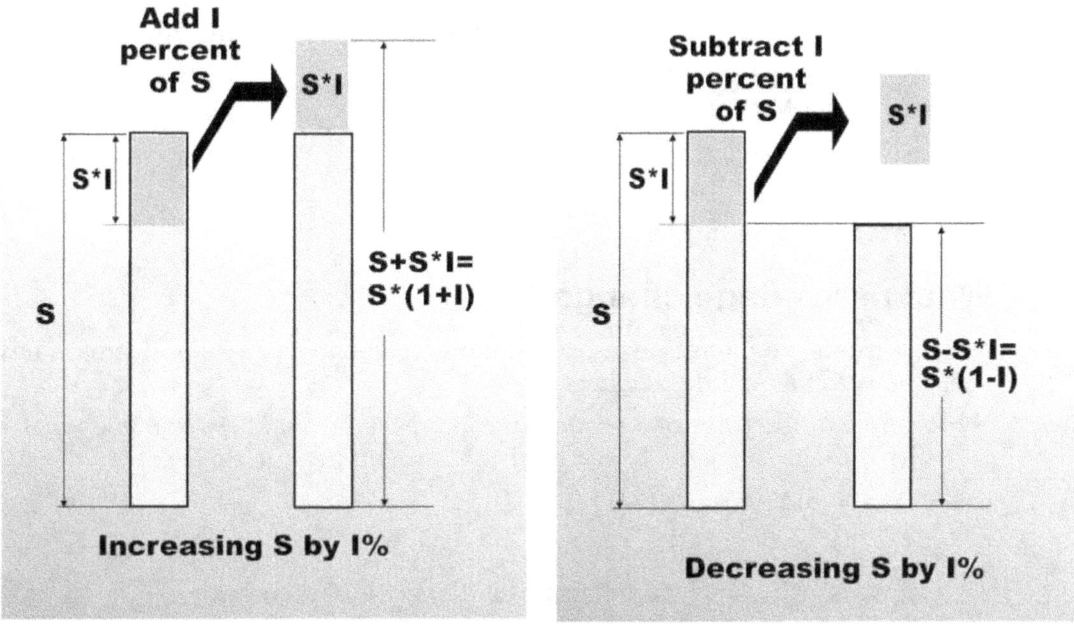

Multiplying to increase and decrease by I%

For example, if you are given a 40% discount, that is the price is decreased by 40% of its original value, then the discounted price is given by multiplying by (1-0.4). If you have to pay a 15% surcharge then the surcharged price is found by multiplying by (1+0.15).

Percentage change at a glance

The use of I, (1+I), (1-I) can be summarized in a table:

Action	Formula
Find I%	=Amount*I
Increase by I%	=Amount*(1+ I)
Decrease by I%	=Amount*(1- I)

Using these formulas you should now find it very easy to work out the effect of a sales tax or value added tax (VAT) on net prices. If the current VAT rate is V% then the gross price can be calculated as:

```
gross price = Net*(1 + V)
```

Similarly if the discount on a price is D% then the discounted price is given by:

```
discounted price = price*(1 - D)
```

What percentage change?

Another interesting question is how much percentage increase or decrease has occurred when a quantity changes.

For example, if the price of a product has increased from $2.50 to $3.00 what is the percentage increase. To work this out all you need to do is solve:

```
new value = old value *(1+I)
```

for I.

That is, working through the steps needed to get I on its own:

1. Multiply out the bracket

    ```
    new value = old value + old value * I
    ```

2. Subtract old value from both sides

    ```
    new value - old value = old value *I
    ```

3. Divide both sides by old value

    ```
    (new value -old value)/old value = I
    ```

This gives:

```
I = (new value - old value)/old value
```

or if you want a more compact version:

```
I = new value/old value - 1
```

The only change needed for a percentage decrease is to put a minus sign in front of the expression:

```
I = 1 - new value/old value
```

In the case of the $2.50 to $3.00 increase the percentage increase is 20%, that is:

```
3.0/2.5 - 1.0 = 0.2
```

Net from Gross

Now to the question of undoing the effect of increasing or decreasing a quantity by a percentage.

If you know the Gross price including tax or other percentage charges and want to know the Net price without it, how do you work it out?

An attractive, but incorrect, line of reasoning is to say that as the Net price (i.e. without tax) was increased by V% to give the Gross price (i.e. with tax) then the Gross price should be decreased by V% to get back to Net.

So a common but incorrect guess is that:

```
Net = Gross*(1 - V)
```

This is misguided because the amount add to Net, i.e. Net*V, isn't the same as the amount subtracted from Gross i.e. Gross*V.

In general if you increase something by I% and then decrease the result by I% you do not get back to where you started!

B2	▼	=	=A2*(1+B1)*(1-B1)
	A	B	C	D
1		50%		
2	200	150		
3				

Increasing 200 by 50% and then decreasing it by 50% results in 150

If you would like a demonstration that this method is incorrect then create the small spreadsheet shown above.

The value entered into A2 is increased by the percentage in B1 and then decreased by the same percentage. You can see in the figure that in the case of 200 and 50% the result is 150 which is very clearly not 200!

If you experiment with this spreadsheet what you will find is that for small values and small percentages the difference between the original value and the calculated value can be quite small and this sometimes leads people to believe that the answer is in fact correct except for a small arithmetic error.

This is of course not true but on occasion the approximation can be useful if you are working things out in your head.

The correct answer depends on a simple rearrangement of the formula:

```
Gross = Net * (1 + V)
```

to give the Net in terms of the Gross:

```
Net = Gross/(1 + V)
```

That is, if you multiply by (1 + V) to get the Gross you have to divide by (1 + V) to get back to the Net.

In general:

- If you know that a value has been increased by I% and you want to calculate the original value divide by (1 + I)
- If you know that a value has been decreased by I% and you want to calculate the original value divide by (1 - I)

Adding percentages

Percentages don't always work in exactly the way that you might think.

The example in the previous section of the erroneous calculation of Net from Gross price should have put you on your guard.

For another example consider the following question - is taking P% of something and then Q% of the result the same as taking P%+Q% of the original value?

Putting this in more practical terms if you are offered a discount of 10% on a price and then offered a further discount of 5% is this the same as a 15% discount?

First let's consider taking successive percentages of something.

Taking P% and then Q% of a value is just:

```
= value * P * Q
```

and this is quite clearly not the same as:

```
= value * (P + Q)
```

To see that this is the case just try a few examples using a spreadsheet and you will quickly discover that the results that the two formulas produce are very different.

For example, if you take 10% of 100, i.e. 10, and then take 20% of this the result is 2, but 10% plus 20%, is 30% and 30% of 100, is 30.

Clearly successive percentages do not add.

In general if you take successive percentages of something they don't add, they multiply.

Going back to our example, taking 10% followed by taking 20% of the result is the same as taking 2% of the original (i.e. 0.1 * 0.2 = 0.02 or 2%).

When reasoning or bargaining with percentages it is usual to speak of "another 1%" in the sense of increasing the percentage offered by adding one percent. In this case it does look as if percentages add but notice that in this particular case all the percentages refer to a proportion of the same whole. That is you are being offered an increase of 1% in the percentage not an additional 1% of what you already have.

In general best way to think about ways of combining percentages is by considering slices of a pie. If you are negotiating for an additional percentage of the whole pie then certainly percentages add, but if you are arguing for a percentage of the slice you have already been allocated then they multiply.

Although mathematically the difference is very obvious it is often lost in the detail of negotiation - on purpose.

A 10% gain and a 10% loss

So in many cases you can be misled by adding percentages. This is also true if you increase or decrease a value by P% and then Q%.

In general:

- Increasing or decreasing a quantity by P% and then Q% is not the same as increasing or decreasing it by (P+Q)%

Consider the 10% discount followed by an additional 5% discount.

In this case the first discount makes the price:

```
= value * (1 - P)
```

and the second takes it to:

```
= value * (1 — P) * (1 - Q)
```

which is clearly not the same as a discount of P+Q percent which would be:

```
= value * (1 — (P + Q))
```

Multiplying out the brackets in the first expression gives:

```
= value * (1 — (P + Q) + P * Q)
```

Comparing the two results indicates that a P% discount followed by an additional Q percent discount gives an overall discount that is smaller by P*Q than a P+Q discount.

The same rule works for percentage increases and a P percent increase followed by a Q percent increase actually gives you an increase of P+Q+P*Q i.e. a bigger percentage increase than P+Q by P*Q.

So a 10% discount followed up by a 5% discount only gives you an overall discount of 14.5% and not the 15% you might expect.

The point here is that it matters whether you are being offered a (10+5)%, i.e. 15% discount, or a 10% discount followed by a further 5%.

This gives us the answer to the discount on a discount problem posed earlier.

Unless you know if the sales person intended to give you a total discount of 15% or alternatively a further discount on the discounted price the actual price you will have to pay isn't clear.

In most cases an additional discount is usually meant in the literal sense of adding to the initial discount - i.e. the intended discount is 10%+5% and not 5% more off the discounted price - what is important is that you realize that there are two possible interpretations.

As another example of how percentages do not add up in the way that you might suppose, consider the following simple problem.

A trader makes a 10% profit on an investment in the first part of the day, but before the day is out has made a 10% loss - is the total profit zero?

The common sense answer to this question is that the 10% gain is wiped out by the 10% loss, but this reasoning does not take into account the fact that the percentages are calculated on different values.

Suppose the initial investment was $100, then a 10% gain is $10 and this makes the total investment worth $110. The following 10% loss reduces the investment by $110*0.1 or $11, making the final investment worth only $99. Hence a 10% gain followed by a 10% loss does not take you back to square one.

Also notice that it does not matter in which order the loss or gain occurred. The answer is exactly the same, a 1% loss on the initial value.

Of course, if both the percentages were quoted relative to the initial investment then the percentages would add up because 10% of $100 is always $10.

Again, what is important here is that you realize that there are two possible meanings and you should always discover what value a percentage change is using as its starting point.

The effective percentage

Often a good way of summarizing a complex transaction which involves different payments and different percentages at different times is to compute a single effective percentage that would be applied to give the same output give the same inputs. The first example of this that we encounter is the use of repeated percentage discounts or charges on a single transaction.

If you are offered a discount of P% and then a further discount of Q% on the discounted price, it is worthwhile asking what actual discount you are receiving on the original price?

This sounds like a difficult question but it is very easy.

The twice the discounted price is given by:

```
price * (1 − P) * (1 - Q)
```

If the total actual discount percentage is D% then the final discounted price is:

```
price * (1 - D)
```

and so:

```
price * (1 − D) = price * (1 − P) * (1 - Q)
```

Canceling price from both sides gives the relationship between Q, P and D:

```
(1 − D) = (1 − P) * (1 - Q)
```

Finally solving for D gives:

```
D = 1 − (1 − P) * (1 - Q)
```

or using the result we got earlier:

```
D = P + Q − P * Q
```

The same is true of percentage increase, but in this case the formula for the actual percentage increase is $(1+P)*(1+Q)-1$. That is, if a value is increased by P% and then the result further increased by Q%, the total percentage increase is:

```
D=(1 + P) * (1 + Q)-1
```

or:

```
D = P + Q + P * Q
```

Which version of the formula to use in any given case is up to you.

For example, if a sales person offers you a further 5% discount on a price that has already been discounted by 10%, the total discount is:

```
1 − (1 − 0.1) * (1 - 0.05)
```

which works out to 14.5% as before.

If you are initially charged 8% extra for a holiday booking and then just before you leave a 15% fuel surcharge is added then the total percentage surcharge is:

```
(1 + 0.08) * (1 + 0.15) - 1
```

or 24.2% increase on the original price.

This is the first and simplest example of an actual or effective percentage. Later when we look at percentages as interest rates we will meet the best known example of actual percentages, the APR or Actual Percentage Rate.

For now let's look at another simpler, but practical, question concerning percentages and interest rates.

Simple tax relief

If you take out a loan at I% interest what is the effective rate if the interest payments are subject to 25% tax relief?

In other words, what rate of interest would result in the same repayments without the tax relief?

We will ignore for the moment questions of repayment, what term the loan is for and the frequency of interest payments. So, if the loan is for M, the interest due each period is simply:

```
M * I
```

If the interest is tax free T% of it would otherwise have been paid to the tax authority and so does not represent an additional outgoing. This reduces the interest payment by T% and makes the effective interest paid only:

```
M * I * (1 - T)
```

and so the effective rate of interest is I * (1 - T)%, i.e. the rate is reduced by T %.

It is interesting to examine the way tax relief changes interest rates and so a simple spreadsheet is called for.

Starting from an empty spreadsheet enter the labels as shown in the spreadsheet below and the following formulas and values:

```
A5  5%
```

```
A6  =A5+0.01
```

```
B5  =A5*(1-$B$1)
```

Copy the formula in A6 into A7..A20 and the formula in B5 into B6..B20. Finally format B1 and A5..B20 as percentages. Note the use of $B$1. This is an absolute cell reference and ensures that copying the formula will not alter it.

This sample table is for a 25% rate of tax. You can, of course, enter any tax rate you want to into cell B1.

	A	B	C
1	Tax rate =	25%	
2			
3	Interest	Effective	
4	rate	rate	
5	5%	3.75%	
6	6.00%	4.50%	
7	7.00%	5.25%	
8	8.00%	6.00%	
9	9.00%	6.75%	
10	10.00%	7.50%	
11	11.00%	8.25%	
12	12.00%	9.00%	
13	13.00%	9.75%	
14	14.00%	10.50%	
15	15.00%	11.25%	
16	16.00%	12.00%	
17	17.00%	12.75%	
18	18.00%	13.50%	
19	19.00%	14.25%	
20	20.00%	15.00%	
21			

Negative percentages

Although we could carry on dealing with percentage increase and decrease as separate cases, it is much simpler to adopt the convention that a positive percentage is an increase and a negative percentage a decrease. In this case to increase/decrease a value by P% you simply multiply by $(1 + P)$ and let the positive and negative signs take care of themselves.

From now on remember:

- A negative percentage corresponds to a percentage decrease and a positive percentage to a percentage increase and in either case we multiply by $(1+P)$.

To see how this simplifies things you only have to look at the formula for the actual percentage which now becomes:

```
(1 + P) * (1 + Q) - 1
```

or:

```
P + Q - P * Q
```

for either an increase and a decrease.

Why do we use percentages?

The use of percentages in many financial situation is so natural that is is worth spending a few moments considering why this is so.

If you need to divide something up into portions so that each person gets an appropriate share of the whole then percentages are a good way to go about it.

If a pie is divided into two parts so that A gets twice as much as B then the appropriate percentages are 66.66...% and 33.33....%. As long as the pie is shared out into these percentages the two-to-one ratio will be maintained.

When relative importance is gauged as a ratio then a percentage allocation is appropriate. However, notice that as the total amount to be divided increases the absolute gap between what A and B each receive increases.

For example, if A and B work for an hourly rate of $20 per hour and $10 per hour, then a percentage wage rise of 10% will keep the two-to-one payment the same at $22 per hour and $11 per hour. However, the differential between the two rates of pay has jumped from $10 to $11. If a percentage increase is repeatedly applied the differential between the hourly rates goes on steadily rising, even though the two-to-one ratio remains unchanged.

This isn't necessarily wrong, but it is important that all concerned understand that a percentage increase or decrease keeps existing ratios fixed but changes absolute differences.

Key points

- A percentage is best entered and stored in a spreadsheet as a decimal fraction. In most spreadsheets this happens automatically if you enter a value followed by a % sign. You can also set a percentage display format to show decimal fractions as percent. That is, entering 33% stores 0.33 in a cell and setting the display format to percent makes it display as 33%.

- If a percentage is stored as a decimal fraction you can work out that percentage of another value simply by multiplying.

- To increase a quantity by I% multiply by (1 + I)

- To decrease a quantity by I% multiply by (1 - I)

- To recover a value that has been increased by I% divide by (1 + I) and to recover a value that has been decreased by I% divide by (1 - I)

- Finding P% of a quantity and then Q% of the result is not the same as finding (P + Q)% of the original value.

- In the same way increasing/decreasing a value by P% and then increasing/decreasing it by Q% is not the same as increasing/decreasing it by (P+Q)%.

- Using a negative percentage to mean a percentage decrease simplifies most formulas involving percentages.

- Percentage increases/decreases maintain existing ratios but change absolute differences in size.

Chapter 2

Time is Money
Simple and Compound Interest

The idea of borrowing money for a specified rate of interest or earning interest on an investment is something that we are all familiar with. Interest is a percentage, but one that has a time-based component. Interest is calculated and paid at a regular intervals and this makes its behavior rather more varied than a simple static percentage.

Interest - a percentage rate

Many financial arrangements are specified in terms of interest which is a percentage of the total per time period.

Interest is a percentage rate - so many percent per month, so many percent per year and so on. It is a rate in the sense of something that involves the passage of time - miles per hour, kilometers per second and 10% per month are all rates.

In the days before legislation tightened up on how interest rates were quoted, it wasn't uncommon to find quotes of 10% interest, but without any mention of the time period involved - and 10% per day is a very different amount of money from 10% per annum.

Thus there are two important components of any interest specification:

    1. The percentage to be paid

    2. The time period governing how often it is paid

This view of percentage as a rate makes clear some of the difficulties in store for us.

For example, if you can make a return of 1% per month, 3% every quarter or 11% per annum, which is the better investment?

A small bank loan is offered at 20% per annum, but a credit card loan costs only 12% per month which is better?

Clearly converting between interest quoted for different time periods is something that we are going to have to examine. But first we need to look at the way that interest is calculated.

Lenders and borrowers

Interest is paid on deposits and charged on loans.

These two situations are in fact identical from the point of view of calculating interest.

In each case there is an investor/lender who provides the lump sum - the principal - and a borrower who pays interest on the loan/investment. It doesn't really matter if the borrower is in fact called a bank, an investment trust or John Smith, the cashflows are the same.

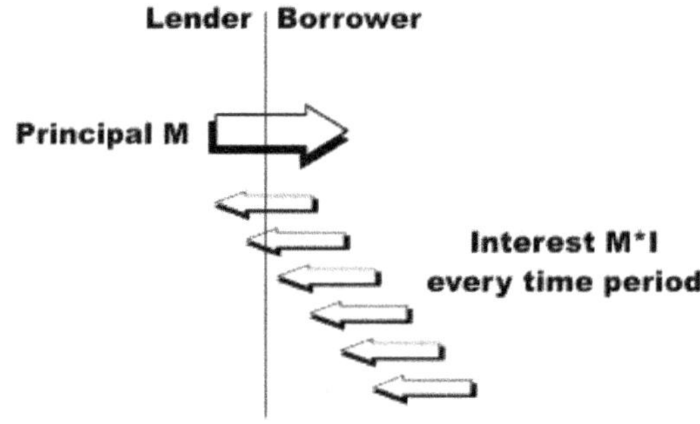

If the principal is $M and the interest rate is I% the interest due each payment period is simply:

=$M * I

Notice that we are not considering the repayment of the loan nor the accumulation of interest.

If the principal is a loan then it is assumed that the whole principal will be paid back as a lump sum sometime in the future - i.e. it is an interest only loan. If the principal is an investment then the interest is paid out to the investor and not reinvested.

The key factor is that the interest is paid in such a way that the value of the principal, i.e. $M, remains constant over time.

In this case the amount of interest paid in each time period is also constant and this results in a very easy to manage situation - simple interest.

Present and Future Value

It is common practice to use the terminology Present Value, or PV, for the sum of money involved at the start of a loan or investment and Future Value, or FV, for the final balance.

In other words, FV is what results after interest has acted on PV.

This jargon applies equally to investments or loans:

- In the case of an investment the amount of money that is deposited or invested is the PV and the final balance is the FV
- In the case of a loan the sum borrowed is the PV and the amount finally paid back is the FV

Other terms, such as principal, are used for PV but for the remainder of this book PV and FV will be used to denote the value before and after the action of interest respectively.

Notice that the relationship between PV and FV depends on the type of situation we are considering.

For example, in the case of simple interest of I% over n interest bearing periods the FV is given by:

```
FV = PV + PV * I * n
```

or:

```
FV = PV * (1 + I * n)
```

You should be able to recognize this as just increasing the PV by I * n%.

Comparing simple interest

In the situation where interest is paid on a PV that does not change over time, it is very easy to compare different interest rates.

For example, if a deposit pays 2% interest per month then over a 12-month period the total amount paid in interest is simply:

```
= PV * 0.02 * 12
```

or:

```
= PV * 0.24
```

This implies that to receive 2% per month is equivalent to receiving 24% per annum.

This same reasoning applies to any interest rate over any time period.

- All we have to do to compare the rates is to convert them to the equivalent rate per annum

For example, 10% paid every six months, i.e. two interest bearing periods per annum, is equivalent to a rate of 0.10*2, i.e. 20% per annum.

In other words, for simple interest rates converting between different periods really is just a matter of multiplying by the ratio of the periods.

For example:

- 0.5%, i.e. half a percent, paid daily is equivalent to 0.5*365% or 185% per annum
- 1% paid bi-monthly is the same as 0.5% paid monthly
- a 50% return over 10 years is equivalent to 5% per annum

Notice that for all of these examples to be correct the situation must correspond to simple interest, i.e. the interest calculated is not added to the PV for the purpose of calculating the next interest payment.

The value of money

Simple though this conversion to an annual rate is, it misses some important points.

In particular, when interest is paid is also an important consideration in determining what it is worth.

Payments made now are generally considered to be worth more than equal payments made in the future. This means that 12 monthly payments are worth more than the same total payment made at the end of the 12-month period.

To understand the why and how of this situation we will have to look more carefully at the way time affects the value of money.

There is also the question of what happens if the interest affects the value of the principal. For example, you may choose to add the interest to the deposit or to increase the debt by deferring interest payments.

This leads us on to consider compound interest.

Compound interest

Most people know that compound interest can exert powerful effects on the value of money, although stories involving a discovered inheritance generated by a small sum invested a long time ago are more often fiction than reality!

Compound interest is at the heart of nearly all financial calculations and it is vital that you understand exactly how it works.

Compound interest arises when the interest generated by a principal is added to the principal rather than being removed from consideration.

- In the case of a loan it corresponds to the interest due being added to the debt, presumably to be paid in full at the end of the loan along with the principal.
- In the case of an investment it corresponds to the interest being added to the investment.
- In both cases the adding of the interest to the principal results in the interest paid changing at each period.

The only difference between an investment and a loan is that in the case of a loan the interest only notionally adds to the amount of money that the borrower actually has. However, this is irrelevant from the lender's point of view because it certainly adds to the size of the debt!

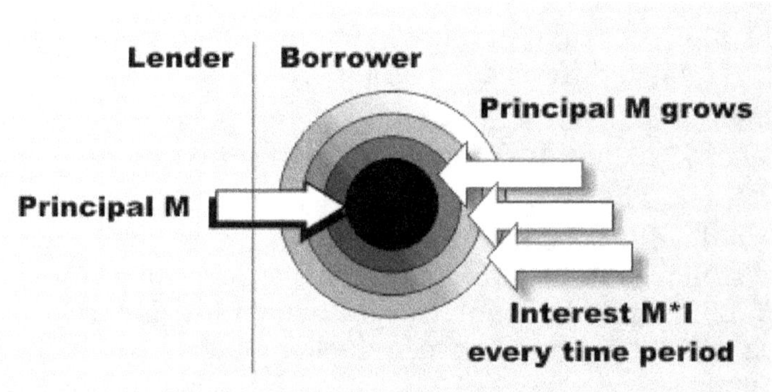

The calculation for compound interest is remarkably simple as long as you have followed and understood the discussion of percentages in Chapter 1.

If the interest is added to the principal this implies that the principal increases by I% in each period. To increase a value by I% you simply multiply by $(1+I)$ and so at the end of the first period the principal, PV, has grown to:

```
= PV * (1 + I)
```

At the end of the second period the principal has grown by another I% and so is given by:

```
= PV * (1 + I) * (1 + I)
```

and so on.

After n periods the principal has increased to M multiplied by $(1+I)$ n times over.

If you repeatedly multiply by the same value n times this is called calculating a power.

Mathematically this operation is indicated as x^n. For example x3 is x*x*x. In the case of spreadsheets calculating a power is indicated either by $x\hat{\ }n$ or $x**n$.

So after n periods the principal is:

```
= PV * (1 + I)ⁿ
```

For example, an investment of $100 at 1% per month would yield a total of 100*0.01*12, i.e. $12, in one year if the interest were taken each month.

If the interest was reinvested each month the total invested at the end of the year would be 100*(1+0.01)^12 which is $112.68, giving a profit of $12.68.

After a single year the difference between simple and compound interest is a mere 68 cents. It hardly seems worth making the effort to do the calculation properly.

However, the difference may start out being small, but compound interest acts to magnify these small differences over time.

So for example, after 20 years the simple interest investment would have earned a total of $240, but the compound interest investment would have earned $989.25.

The reason for the difference can be seen in the figure below, which shows a graph of the earnings for the two investments against time. You can see that the compound interest calculation causes the earning due to interest to increase each year. So the gap between the two widens, gradually at first, and then more rapidly.

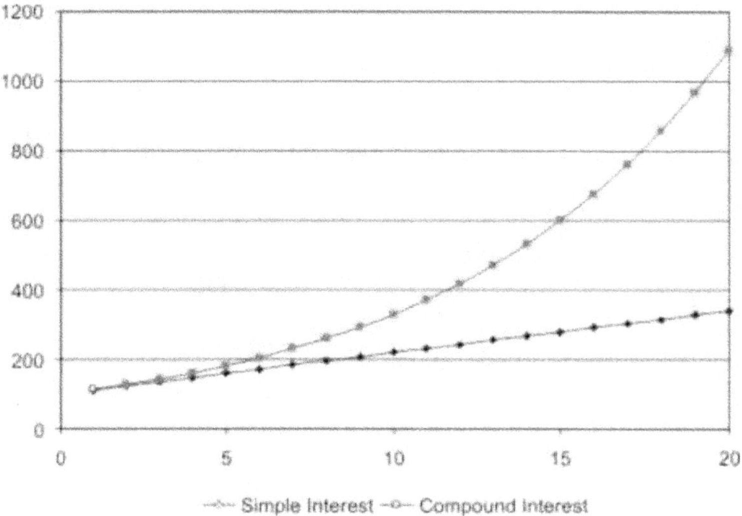

Financial functions

In the days before computers, calculations involving compound interest were considered to be very difficult. Working out powers and performing the necessary multiplications was time consuming and error prone. To reduce the burden tables and calculating approximations were often employed and an air of mysticism often surrounded financial calculations.

With a spreadsheet however there is no need to to fear any calculation - working out a power is just as easy as a multiplication.

In most spreadsheets Future Value (FV) can be calculated using a function like:

```
=FV(I,n,0,-PV)
```

where the principal is invested for n compounding periods at I% per period.

Notice that there is a minus sign in front of PV. It is a convention that cash paid in (e.g. PV) is negative while cash paid out (e.g. FV) is positive.

Don't worry about the 0 included in the function. In more complicated examples it represents any periodic savings you might make in addition to the lump sum initial value PV.

For example, $100 invested for 5 years at 4% per annum produces a final balance of $121.67.

The formula to type into a spreadsheet to calculate this is:

```
=FV(4%,5,0,-100)
```

If you prefer to express the interest rate as a decimal fraction it becomes:

```
=FV(0.04,5,0,-100)
```

Notice the minus sign in front of the initial value. As explained earlier, this is because this represents cash that has been paid in.

The above formula works out compound interest that is added on an annual basis.

If you are being paid monthly interest you have to divide the annual interest rate by 12 to give a monthly rate and multiply the number of periods by 12 to give the number of months:

```
=FV(4%/12,5*12,0,-100)
```

Similarly if interest is added daily the formula to use is:

```
=FV(4%/365,5*365,0,-100)
```

- The golden rule is that the interest rate must always be correct for the compounding period.

In fact the compounding period can make quite a difference as shown in the figure which shows the formulas to enter as well as the results:

	A	B	C
1	$100 invested at 4% for 5 years:		
2	Compounded	Formula	Return
3	Annually	=FV(4%,5,0,-100)	$121.67
4	Monthly	=FV(4%/12,5*12,0,-100)	$122.10
5	Daily	=FV(4%/365,5*365,0,-100	$122.14

The effect of different compounding periods

Solving for I, PV or n

The standard compound interest formula calculates the final balance produced when a given sum, the principal or PV, is invested at a given interest rate, I, for a given number of years, n.

Often this is exactly what you want to know, but sometimes financial questions are best put in terms of the interest rate or the investment term required.

For example, if I need a return of $1000 in 10 years time how much do I need to invest assuming I can secure an 8% interest rate for the full 10 years?

To answer this and other similar questions what we need are three other rearrangements of the standard compound interest formula to give n, I and PV respectively. For such a simple calculation these formulas are surprisingly difficult to work out because they involve manipulating powers. However what really matters is what the formula are and this can be seen in the table below along with equivalent financial functions:

To calculate	Formula	Spreadsheet Function
Return (FV)	`PV*(1+I)^n`	`=FV(I,n,0,-PV)`
Interest Rate (I%)	`(FV/PV)^(1/n)-1`	`=RATE(n,0,-PV,FV)`
Term (n) in years	`ln(FV/PV)/ln(1+I)`	`=NPER(I,0,-PV,FV)`
Investment (PV)	`FV*(1+I)^-n`	`=PV(I,n,0,FV)`

The only unusual component of the formulas given is the use of the ln (log natural) function in calculating n. If you haven't encountered this function before don't worry too much about it because all spreadsheets support the LN function, so you can just use it.

To return to the problem at the beginning of this section, but slightly rephrased:

What does PV have to be if FV is $1000, I is 8% per annum with interest added monthly and the investment period is 10 years?

The answer is;

```
=1000*(1+0.08/12)^(-10*12)
```

or using the PV function:

```
=PV(8%/12,10*12,0,1000)
```

Both work out to be $450.52.

You can check this by working out the FV of $450.52 at 8% per annum calculated monthly for 10 years:

```
=450.52*(1+0.08/12)^(10*12)
```

or using the FV function:

```
=FV(8%/12,10*12,0,450.52)
```

which gives $999.99 or thereabouts.

The exact result depends on the number of digits precision that your spreadsheet works to, but 1 cent in $1000 in ten years isn't an unacceptable error.

An investment/loan spreadsheet

It is very convenient to have a spreadsheet that you can use to calculate the unknown fourth quantity involved in an investment or loan given any three of them. This is very easy using the formulas listed in the table above. Follow along to create this spreadsheet for yourself in Excel, LibreOffice Calc or as a Google Sheet so that you can experiment with different values or skip to the next section if you don't want the hands-on experience.

A column of entered values can be created next to a column of formulas that calculate each value from the remaining three. This description is easier to understand with reference to the screen dump below:

	A	B	C
		Entered	Calculated
1			
2	Investment (PV)	$100.00	£100.00
3	Annual Interest Rate	5%	5.00%
4	Term (in years)	5	5.00
5	Return (FV)	$128.34	£128.34
6			

Enter the labels in column A and in B1 and C1 as shown, but do not enter any values in column B yet.

The formulas in the following table need to be entered into column C:

Calculate	Cell	Formula
Investment PV	C2	`=PV(B3/12,B4*12,0,-B5)`
Interest Rate	C3	`=RATE(B4*12,0,-B2,B5)*12`
Term in years	C4	`=NPER(B3/12,0,-B2,B5)/12`
Return FV	C5	`=FV(B3/12,B4*12,0,-B2)`

Notice the need to multiply by 12 to convert the calculated monthly rate into a per annum rate and to divide by 12 to convert the term in months into years.

The final touch is to format B2:C2 and B5:C5 as currency and B3:C3 as percentage with two decimal places. Now when you enter any three of the values into column B the fourth will be calculated in column C.

Initially, because we have not typed anything in column B for the "Entered" values, when the spreadsheet attempts to work out the Calculated values, the resulting is a mix of zeros and error messages.

This highlights a problem with this spreadsheet - as we only want it to work out one formula at a time the unused ones will show spurious results or suggest there are errors due to the incomplete data in column B.

The solution is to test if each entered value is zero and only calculate a value if it is, on the assumption that if the user hasn't supplied one then it must be needed. This means surrounding the formulas in column C with IF statements that do the calculation when the cell to the left is zero and display a blank cell otherwise.

Calculate	Cell	Formula
Investment PV	C2	`=IF(B2=0,PV(B3/12,B4*12,0,-B5),"")`
Interest Rate	C3	`=IF(B3=0,RATE(B4*12,0,-B2,B5)*12,"")`
Term in years	C4	`=IF(B4=0,NPER(B3/12,0,-B2,B5)/12,"")`
Return FV	C5	`=IF(B5=0,FV(B3/12,B4*12,0,-B2),"")`

Now once three quantities are entered the remaining one will be calculated as shown below.

	A	B	C
1		Entered	Calculated
2	Investment (PV)	$100.00	
3	Annual Interest Rate	5%	
4	Term (in years)		5.00
5	Return (FV)	$128.34	
6			

An affordable loan

Although there is a tendency to think of this spreadsheet and its related calculations in terms of investment where the interest is re-invested, it is worth keeping in mind that it also applies to loans where the interest is `rolled up' into the total debt to be repaid.

For example, if you know that you can afford to repay $1000 (and presumably make a reasonable profit) at the end of a 3-year project, how much can you borrow at 20% per annum.

Using the spreadsheet with FV equal to $1000 quickly gives the answer $551.53.

Inflation

Inflation is the gradual erosion of the purchasing power of money.

As this is usually reported as a percentage rate per annum it has many of the properties of compound interest. However while compound interest normally works to increase the size of the principal, inflation generally reduces the value of the principal.

For example, if inflation is running at 10% per annum, $100 held at the start of the year will be worth only $90 at the start of the next year. At this point it is tempting to use the simplistic argument that the $90 will be further reduced by $10 in the following year and so on until after 10 years there will be no value left at all!

This is clearly incorrect but it is surprising how often the argument is encountered.

The correct reasoning is. of course, that in the second year the value is reduced by 10% of $90, which is only $9 not a further $10 and so on..

You can see how inflation acts like compound interest in that the reduction in value affects the next time period's calculation. To be more exact, after one year the value of $M is:

```
=M*(1-I)
```

after two years it is:

```
=M*(1-I)*(1-I)
```

and after *n* years it is:

```
=M*(1-I)^n
```

This is of course just the general formula for the FV under compound interest but with -I instead of +I. If we regard inflation as a negative interest rate then we can use all of the formulas listed earlier without change to calculate the effect of inflation.

For example, what will be the value of $100 in ten years time in today's terms if inflation is running at 3% per annum? The answer is simply:

```
=100*(1-0.03)^10
```

or:

```
=FV(-3%,10,0,-100)
```

Both of these work out to $73.74.

That is, with 3% inflation, in 10 years time $100 will only buy what $73.74 will buy today.

Notice that in the case of inflation there is a potential for confusion over the use of the terms Future Value and Present Value!

There is a subtle point in the previous calculation that has been ignored so far. The annual rate of inflation may be quoted as 8% per annum but what is the compounding period?

The answer is that it depends on how the quoted rate has been calculated. Inflation is a process that happens continuously and so there is no sensible or reasonable compounding period to choose for calculations. (This point is discussed in more detail in Chapter 3). In most cases the quoted rate gives the correct results for an annual compounding period, hence the calculations above. This is often referred to as the "year-on-year inflation rate".

Half-life of money

To give you an example of how the other compound interest formulas can be used how would you calculate the number of years it takes for the value of money to exactly halve, given any particular inflation rate? This is just a matter of using formulas that give LN in terms of PV, FV and I.

That is, time to half-value is:

`=LN(PV/2PV)/LN(1+I)`

which simplifies to:

`=LN(1/2)/LN(1+I)`

or using the NPER function:

`=NPER(-I%,0,-PV,PV/2)`

For example, if inflation is 6% then the number of years to halve the value is:

`=LN(0.5)/LN(1-0.06)`

or using the NPER function and a nominal present value of $100:

`=NPER(-6%,0,-100,100/2)`

both of which work out to 11.2 years.

Notice that it is important to remember that the inflation rate is treated as a negative rate in all of the compound interest formulas - hence the -0.06 or -6% in the above.

The time it takes inflation to reduce the value of currency to 50% of its original value could be called the `half life' because it is exactly analogous to the definition of the half life of radioactive elements. How the inflation rate determines monetary half life is quite a useful way of trying to gain an understanding of the effects of inflation.

It is quite easy to construct a spreadsheet that tabulates half-life.
Enter the labels and data as shown in column A and B1.

Type the formula:

```
=LN(0.5)/LN(1-A2)
```

into B2 and copy it down the column.

	A	B
1	Inflation	Half life
2	1%	68.97
3	2%	34.31
4	3%	22.76
5	4%	16.98
6	5%	13.51
7	6%	11.20
8	7%	9.55
9	8%	8.31
10	9%	7.35
11	10%	6.58
12	11%	5.95
13	12%	5.42
14	13%	4.98
15	14%	4.60
16	15%	4.27
17	16%	3.98
18	17%	3.72
19	18%	3.49
20	19%	3.29
21	20%	3.11
22		

The half-life of money

It also helps to examine the half-life using a graph. This makes it quite clear that the largest changes in half-life occur when the inflation rate is small. With inflation running at 10% or more money loses half its value in less than 7 years and if the inflation rate hits 30% it halves the value of money in less than 2 years.

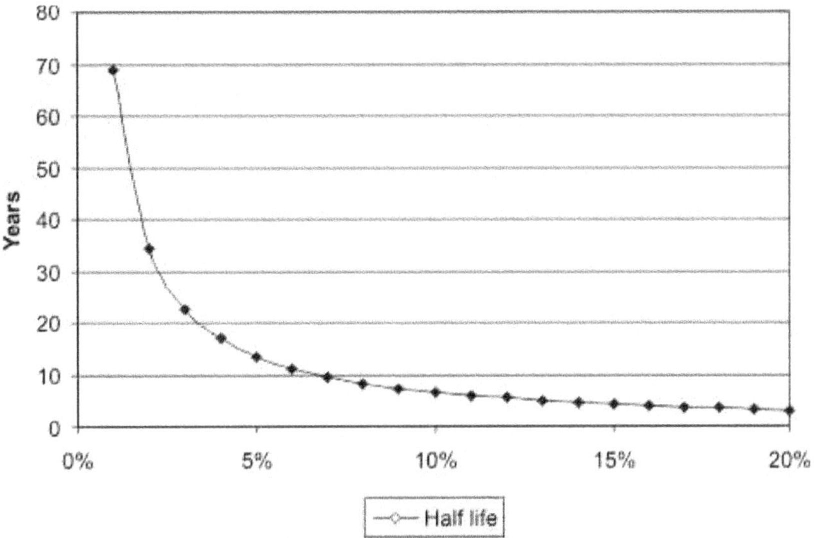

The half-life of money during inflation

Inflation and interest

It is obvious that inflation and interest pull the value of an investment or loan in different directions.

To make a true appraisal of value it is important to look at inflation adjusted estimates of FV. Notice that when it comes to interest it is possible for the calculation to be exact and determinate but but once inflation is considered we really are dealing with estimates of worth.

Fortunately the calculations are very easy. If you invest PV at I% for Y years compounded monthly then the FV is:

```
=PV * (1 + I/12)^(Y * 12)
```

If inflation is running at F% per annum the FV will only be worth:

```
=FV * (1 - F)^Y
```

Putting these two together gives the estimate of FV in today's terms as:

```
=PV * (1 + I/12)^(Y * 12) * (1 - F)^Y
```

Although this looks like a very complicated formula you can easily make use of it in a spreadsheet to calculate the effects of inflation on an investment or loan.

Notice that, as pointed out in Chapter 1, percentages and percentage rates do not add. So for example, an interest rate of 10% coupled with an inflation rate of 2% doesn't produce an effective rate of 8% - but you will still often hear, and even read, this sort of reasoning!

Another common error is to assume that if inflation is running at 10%, say, then an interest rate of exactly 10% will offset its effects. This is another example, of the 10% decrease canceling a 10% increase discussed in Chapter 1 and it is as wrong when applied to interest rates as when it is applied to percentages!

If inflation is running at x% then an interest rate of x% still results in an overall loss of value of a deposit. If you would like to investigate this statement for yourself then you need the following spreadsheet.

Investments and loans with inflation

Using the standard compound interest formulas it is easy to put together a spreadsheet that will tabulate the real gain on an investment over any time period.

	A	B	C	
1	Investment	$1,000.00		
2	Interest	8%		
3	Inflation	4%		
4				
5	Years	FV	FV adjusted	
6		1 $1,083.00	$1,039.68	
7		2 $1,172.89	$1,080.93	
8		3 $1,270.24	$1,123.82	
9		4 $1,375.67	$1,168.42	
10		5 $1,489.85	$1,214.78	
11		6 $1,613.50	$1,262.98	
12		7 $1,747.42	$1,313.10	
13		8 $1,892.46	$1,365.20	
14		9 $2,049.63	$1,419.37	
15		10 $2,219.64	$1,475.69	
16		11 $2,403.87	$1,534.24	
17		12 $2,603.39	$1,595.12	
18		13 $2,819.47	$1,658.42	
19		14 $3,053.48	$1,724.22	
20		15 $3,306.92	$1,792.64	
21				

First enter the text and values shown in column A and row 5.

The formula:

```
=$B$1*(1+$B$2/12)^(A6*12)
```

should be entered into B6 and copied into B7..B20.

The formula:

```
=B6*(1-$B$3)^A6
```

should be entered into C6 and copied into C7..C20. Cells B1 and B6..C20 should be set to currency format and B3 and B4 to percentage format.

Notice the use of absolute cell references in the formula. Also notice that the FV adjusted for inflation has been calculated in two stages rather than using the full formula given earlier. It is often better to break a complicated calculation down into smaller stages that can be checked and edited more easily.

You can, of course extend this spreadsheet to cover any number of years simply by copying the formulas into additional rows. Once again notice that this calculation applies to loans as well as investments. In either case it is the borrower rather than the lender who benefits. For example, in the situation shown in the screen dump if the principal was borrowed at 8% per annum to be repaid in full including interest in 15 years then, although the paper value of the repayment is $3307, it should only `feel like' $1793. Thus inflation erodes debt as well as wealth! Of course the results of this spreadsheet have to be interpreted carefully because they depend on the estimated value of future inflation.

While you might be confident about future interest rates, inflation is a far less controllable quantity. In practice inflation will vary over the period of the calculation and so the results are only approximate, even if you use an estimate of the average inflation. Inflation is discussed again in more detail in a later chapter.

Key points

- Interest is a percentage rate and its specification involves a percentage and a time period.

- Simple interest is where the interest earned or owed is not added to the sum invested or borrowed and so doesn't affect the period interest calculation.

- For simple interest $FV=PV*(1+n*I\%)$ where FV is the Future Value, PV is the Present value, I% the interest rate and n is the number of interest bearing periods.

- To convert from an annual rate of interest to a monthly rate simply divide by 12. Conversions between rates over other periods follow a similar method.

- Compound interest is where the interest earned or owed is added to the sum invested or borrowed and so does affect the subsequent interest calculations.

- Spreadsheets have a range of financial functions which can be used to simplify the raw formulas involved in interest calculations.

- Inflation is an application of compound interest that reduces rather than increases the value of money.

Formula summary

This chapter has introduced a number of formulas to calculate simple and compound interest. The following tables gives the formulas and functions that provide the relationships between the sum invested, PV; the future return, FV; the rate of interest, I%; over n, the number of compounding periods.

To calculate:	Formula	Spreadsheet Function
Simple interest		
FV (Return)	`= PV *(1 + n*I)`	N/A
I% (Rate)	`=((FV/PV)-1)/n`	N/A
n periods	`=((FV/PV)-1)/I`	N/A
PV (Investment)	`=FV/(1 + n*I)`	N/A
Compound interest		
FV (Return)	`=PV*(1 + I)^n`	`=FV(I,n,0,-PV)`
I% (Rate)	`=(FV/PV)^(1/n)-1`	`=RATE(n,0,-PV,FV)`
n periods	`=ln(FV/PV)/ln(1 + I)`	`=NPER(I,0,-PV,FV)`
PV (Investment)	`=FV*(1 + I)^-n`	`=PV(I,n,0,FV)`

Chapter 3

Effective Interest Rate

In the previous chapter we discovered that compound interest is nothing more than the repeated application of simple interest to the accumulated total of the principal and the interest to date. This is such a common form of financial transaction that we tend to treat it as something special. In particular, we like to summarize the effect that compounding has on the underlying or nominal interest rate.

This leads us to the idea of the `effective' annual interest rate and then on the formalized Effective Interest Rate or Annual Percentage Rate, the much quoted EIR/APR.

As well as changes to effective rates due to compounding, there is also the question of how the effect of tax and tax allowances can be summarized within an interest rate. This brings us to the idea of nett and gross rates. Finally we consider some issues of working with different compounding periods.

The effective rate

If you make an investment with the interest reinvested then it is clear that the effect of compounding will result in you being paid more interest at the end of the year than the simple nominal annual rate would suggest. For example, if you invest $100 at a nominal rate of 10% per annum compounded monthly, at the end of one year you will have earned $110.47, not the $110 that the nominal interest might lead you to believe.

Because of compounding the effective interest rate per annum appears to be 10.47% and this is what a Bank or other institution might consider is the annual interest worth quoting because it allows for the compounding that will almost certainly occur. This is the effective, or actual, annual rate of interest that applies to an investment - as long as the interest isn't withdrawn each month. The same sort of reasoning applies to loans. In this case the effective or actual rate of annual interest applies if the interest on the debt is rolled up into the amount borrowed and hence owed. If you pay the interest on the loan monthly then the rate that applies is the nominal rate.

The effective rate is also often quoted as 'so many percent compound' as in 10.9% per annum compound. This method of presentation makes it quite clear that what is being quoted is a rate that results if and only if you leave the interest to attract further interest.

Also notice that in this case it isn't even important that the compounding period is quoted. What is at issue is the effective rate.

Calculating the effective rate

Clearly the effective, or actual, annual interest rate is an important quantity and it is worth knowing how to calculate it in general.

The value of the investment at the end of one year is simply the future value and so the total amount earned in interest is the future value minus the present value.

Putting this another way the Future Value FV is related to the Present Value by:

```
FV=(1 + EI) * PV
```

This is the fundamental equation of finance. The FV can always be regarded as the PV increased by EI% in one interest earning period. If you know the FV and the PV you can rearrange the equation to five the interest rate - the effective interest rate over a single investment period.

That is:

```
effective annual rate = EI = (FV-PV)/PV
```

or

```
=FV/PV-1
```

Now you can use the fact that the FV is given by the application of the monthly interest rate:

```
FV = PV *(1 + I)^n
```

This gives a formula that connects I, the monthly rate, and EI, the effective annual rate:

```
EI = PV *(1 + I)^n / PV -1
```

If you want to you can make use of this formula directly in a spreadsheet although it isn't the most efficient way of doing the calculation.

If you try it out you will discover that you get the same result no matter what PV is. This is entirely reasonable because there is no reason why the effective annual rate should depend on the present value.

If you set PV to $1 (or by writing the formula out in full and canceling out the principal) then you get a the simplest formula possible for the effective annual rate:

```
=(1+I)^n-1
```

where I is the interest rate per compounding period and n is the number of periods in one year.

As the most common compounding period is one month, the relation between the nominal annual rate and the effective annual rate is:

```
A = (1 + I/12)^12-1
```

where I is the nominal annual interest rate and A the effective or actual annual rate.

For example, if the nominal annual interest rate for savings is 10% and the interest is calculated and added monthly then the effective annual rate is:

```
(1 + 0.01/12)^12-1
```

This works out to 10.47% after rounding to two decimal places.

The effective annual rate is also called the Compounded Annual Rate or CAR.

If you need to work out the nominal annual rate given the effective annual rate, i.e. to go back to the rate before compounding, this is:

```
I = ((I + A)^1/12-1)*12
```

Nominal and effective

In case you are getting lost in all of this discussion of nominal and effective interest rates, a summary might prove useful:

- The nominal rate of interest is the rate without taking the effect of compounding into account.
- To convert from the annual nominal rate to the rate that is applied at each calculation and addition of interest, simply divide by the number of interest periods in a year.
- If the interest paid is added to the principal then the effect of compound interest can be summarized in the effective annual rate.

Looked at yet another way, the effective annual rate tells you by what percentage the principal will grow in a year taking compounding into account.

An effective rate spreadsheet

The conversion of nominal to effective rate is difficult enough to warrant a spreadsheet devoted to it.

First enter the text as shown in column A.

B5		▼	=	=(1+B3/B4)^B4-1

	A	B
1	Annual rate conversion	
2		
3	Nominal annual rate	5.00%
4	Compounding periods per annum	12
5	Calculated effective annual rate	5.12%
6		
7	Effective annual rate	5.12%
8	Compounding periods per annum	12
9	Calculated nominal annual rate	5.00%
10		

Next enter the formula:

```
=(1+B3/B4)^B4-1
```

in cell B5 and:

```
=((1+B7)^(1/B8)-1)*B8
```

in cell B9 and set percentage formats with two decimal places on B3, B5, B7 and B9. Don't worry that you see #DIV/0! in the cells where the formulas are entered - this is just because no valid data has been entered for the formulas to work on.

For most rate calculations the compounding period will be a month, making B4 and B8 almost permanently set to 12. If you enter the nominal rate into B3 then the effective rate will be calculated in B5. If you enter the effective rate in to B7 then the nominal rate will be calculated in B9.

Nominal to effective converter

Another useful spreadsheet is one that shows the effective annual rate for a range of nominal annual rates. This is very simple to construct.

First enter the labels shown in in row 1 of screen dump. Next enter the nominal percentage rates 1% to 30% in column A. Enter the formula to calculate the effective rate:

```
=(1+A2/12)^12-1
```

into B2 and the formula to calculate the difference between the nominal and effective rate into C2:

```
=B2-A2
```

Set both these cells to display in percentage format with two decimal places and copy them into B3..C31.

B5		= =(1+A5/12)^12-1	
	A	B	C
1	Nominal rate	Effective rate	Difference
2	1%	1.00%	0.00%
3	2%	2.02%	0.02%
4	3%	3.04%	0.04%
5	4%	4.07%	0.07%
6	5%	5.12%	0.12%
7	6%	6.17%	0.17%
8	7%	7.23%	0.23%
9	8%	8.30%	0.30%
10	9%	9.38%	0.38%
11	10%	10.47%	0.47%
12	11%	11.57%	0.57%
13		12.68%	.9%

Notice the way that the difference between the nominal and effective rate increases as the nominal rate increases. You can see this more clearly by creating an X-Y chart with Nominal rate (column A) on the X-axis and Difference (column C) on the Y-axis as shown below.

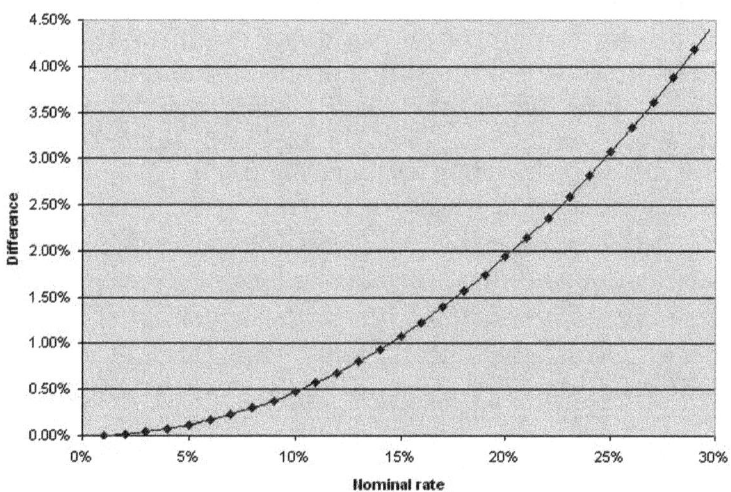

The EIR - Effective Interest Rate

The use of the effective rate is enshrined in legislation in many countries but both the law and the terminology used varies. For example in the USA the term APR is used to refer to the nominal Annual Percentage Rate i.e. without taking compounding into account but in the UK the same term, APR, refers to the Annual Percentage Rate which does take compounding (and other one off payments) into account. You can see that confusion is not only possible but likely in reading any financial document. Your only hope of getting things right is to understand what is being calculated.

In general, the term Effective Interest Rate (EIR) is used to refer to the general concept of including compounding in the quoted rate but this is sometimes called by other names, for example APR (Annual Percentage Rate) in the UK. As we already know the formula to convert nominal to effective rate, you might think that there is very little more to say about EIR, but in fact there is a great deal. The reason is simply that there are different forms of loan involving different repayment schemes, such as regular payments or single payments, and the effect of additional charges to consider.

However in one very simple situation - where the interest is simply calculated on the balance at a periodic interval - we do indeed know how to calculate the EIR. More complex loans will be covered in a later chapter.

Credit card EIR/APR

Although the EIR/APR has to be quoted for a great many types of loan, the most commonly encountered is the credit card. In this case the nominal interest rate is quoted as a monthly rate and conversion has to be made to an effective annual rate.

For example, if an interest rate of 1% per month is quoted, the nominal annual rate (the APR in the USA) is 12% while the effective annual rate (the APR in many countries and the EIR in the USA) is 12.6825%. Similarly a 2% per month nominal rate is equal to an EIR/APR of 26.8%. It is very important to notice that this simple calculation assumes that there are no charges other than the monthly percentage quoted.

Cards that charge fixed annual fees and cash advances which attract a single surcharge have an EIR/APR that is calculated by slightly more complicated methods.

A spreadsheet to calculate the EIR/APR on the monthly rate is easy enough to construct. Enter the text and labels shown in the screen dump into column A and enter the formula to calculate the effective annual rate from the monthly nominal rate:

```
=(1+B4)^12-1
```

into B5.

B5	▼	=	=(1+B4)^12-1

	A	B
1	**Credit Card APR**	
2	Note: only valid for credit cards that do not charge a monthly fee	
3		
4	Monthly rate	1.65%
5	Effective rate	21.699%
6	APR (UK) =	21.60%
7		

In the UK the effective rate has to be truncated to one decimal place to be called the APR and this is worth calculating because it demonstrates how to truncate a percentage in general.

Truncating a percentage

For this we need the function:

`TRUNC(val,n)`

which simply chops off the decimal places in *val* to leave just *n* digits after the decimal point.

You might think that you need:

`TRUNC(val,1)`

However, if you remember that percentages are actually stored as decimal fractions you should be able to see that the correct formula is:

`TRUNC(val,3)`

For example, 52.13% is in fact stored as 0.5213 and truncating this to three decimal places gives 0.521, which displays as 52.1%. So truncating a percentage to one decimal place corresponds to truncating the equivalent decimal fraction to three decimal places.

In the spreadsheet above the correct formula is

`=TRUNC(B5,3)`

which should be entered into B6.

Effective rate - a broader view

There is a tendency to think of the effective rate of interest as something that relates only to the way compounding increases the effect of an annual rate of interest applied monthly - but this is just the one manifestation of the way compounding can affect a simple interest rate.

In all transactions the fundamental quantity is the simple interest rate - the percentage per time period. The fundamental calculation is always the trivial one of simple interest per time period.

For example, if an investment earns I% per month then at the end of one month the amount has grown to:

```
FV=PV*(1+I)
```

where PV is the amount on deposit for the month concerned.

If the same amount is on deposit for n months the final sum could be calculated by using the simple interest formula n times. Alternatively we can use a shortcut formula:

```
FV=PV*(1+I)^n
```

In this sense compound interest calculations have to be seen as a shortcut to obtaining the result that the repeated application of simple interest would give.

Notice that if the amount on deposit each month varies then the compound interest calculation cannot be used and there is no alternative but to use the simple interest calculation using the amount on deposit at the end of each month.

When the amount on deposit changes in a regular and predictable way, for example in an annuity where a fixed sum is withdrawn each time period, then there are shortcut methods of calculation similar to compound interest and these are described in later chapters.

The effective rate is also a shortcut way of working out the effect that compounding has on the nominal or simple interest rate. If you deposit PV for n periods at a nominal/simple interest rate of I% then the future value is given by:

```
FV=PV*(1+I)^n
```

The effective interest rate, E%, is just the simple interest rate that gives the same future value. That is:

`FV=PV*(1+E)=PV*(1+I)^n`

which if you compare the two gives

`E=(1+I)^n-1`

which is the fundamental relationship between nominal and effective rates derived earlier for an annual rate applied monthly, i.e. with *n* equal to 12.

This more general form of effective interest rate allows the effect of compounding over any period to be summarized as a simple interest rate.

For example, if you deposit $100 at 10% per annum paid yearly the annual nominal and effective interest rates are the same because there is no compounding. However if you leave, or plan to leave, the deposit untouched for 10 years then annual compounding produces a future value of:

`FV=100*(1+0.1)^10 = $259.37`

and the effective interest rate for a 10-year period is:

`E=(1+0.1)^10-1 = 1.5937`

or 159.37% per 10 years.

If you would like to check these figures try calculating the future value as simple interest using the effective rate, that is:

`FV=100*(1+1.5937)`
`  =$259.37`

As you can see, the effective rate gives the same future value using a simple interest calculation as compound interest calculated using the nominal rate.

In general:

- the effective rate is the simple interest equivalent of a rate that is compounded over a given number of periods
- to find the effective rate write down the formula for the compounded rate and a simple interest formula for the same time period. Solve for the simple interest rate that gives the same future value.

The same ideas hold for a loan as for an investment.

More than one year

Given that by now you understand the idea of effective rate fully, you might like to consider the following question before you read on.

A deposit attracts 10% per annum compounded monthly, giving an effective annual rate of 10.47%. If the deposit is left undisturbed for five years what is the future value?

The future value at the end of one year can be calculated using simple interest and the effective annual rate of 10.47%, that is:

```
FV= 100*(1+0.1047)
  = $110.47
```

The question is, can the simple interest calculation be used to give the Future Value after five years using five times the effective rate?

The answer is obviously no because there is now another compounding effect to take into account. The interest at the end of each year itself earns interest and this is not taken into account in the effective rate.

The point is that the effective rate is an annual rate and only summarizes the influence of a single year's compounding. You can still use the annual effective rate to calculate the Future Value after five years but only by using the compound interest formula:

```
FV= 100*(1+0.1047)^5
  = $164.52
```

which of course gives the same result as using the monthly interest rate for the entire 10 years:

```
FV= 100*(1+0.1/12)^(5*12)
  = $164.53
```

The difference of 1 cent is within the accuracy of the calculation. If the effective annual rate had been used to more decimal places then the results would have tallied more closely. The point is that the effective interest rate summarizes the effect that compounding has over a specified period.

In the example above, the effective rate summarizes the monthly compounding to give a yearly rate, but if you want to calculate what happens in subsequent years you must remember to use the compound interest formula?

The compounding period

If you were offered an investment rate of 10% per annum compounded monthly, weekly or daily which would you choose?

The answer should be obvious after only a few moments' thought.

The more frequent the compounding the higher the effective rate. For example the effective rate of 10% compounded monthly is:

```
(1+0.1/12)^12-1 = 10.47131%
```

but 10% compounded daily is:

```
(1+0.1/365)^365-1 = 10.515%
```

Of course daily isn't the upper limit and higher effective rates could be achieved by compounding more often than once a day.

If you allow the compounding to be performed so often that it can be considered to be continuous then the form of the equation giving the effective rate of interest changes to:

```
effective rate = EXP(I)-1
```

Most spreadsheets have an EXP or exponential function so working out the effective rate due to continuous compounding is relatively easy. In maths books you will also see the same formula written as:

$$e^i-1$$

where e is the exponential number roughly equal to 2.71828. The spreadsheet function =EXP(I) is identical to e^I.

Using this formula for continuous compounding gives the effective annual interest rate for 10% as:

```
=EXP(0.1)-1=10.517%
```

which you can see is bigger than all of the effective rates that we have calculated so far. Of course this is no accident because by continuously compounding the nominal rate we reach the largest effective rate possible.

If you want to calculate the Future Value of an investment at any time *t* then the appropriate formula is;

```
FV=PV*EXP(t*I)
```

Notice that if I is an annual rate then t has to be in years and fractions of years, e.g. t=1.5 is 1 year 6 months.

Where does the exp come from?

It is something of a mystery how the formula for compound interest changes its form so completely.

Unfortunately the reason depends on some fairly technical looking mathematics. You don't have to understand the contents of this section to make use of the exponential functions, but it is interesting.

The future value of an investment earning I% per annum compounded *n* times per year is:

```
(1+I/n)^(t*n)
```

where *t* is the fraction of a year that has passed.

For example, if *n* is 365, i.e. daily compounding, then the future value after half a year is:

```
(1+I/365)^(0.5*n)
```

If n is increased the number of compounding periods increase and the larger n becomes the closer we approach continuous compounding. In mathematical terms we need to investigate the form of the equation as n, the number of compounding periods per year, tends to infinity.

It turns out to be easier find the limit in terms of the new quantity n' which is the number of compounding periods divided by the interest rate that is

```
n'=n/I
```

and so

```
n=n'*I
```

Rewriting the formula in terms of n' gives:

```
(1+1/n')^(n'*I*t)
```

Now you can see the advantage of the new quantity n' because we can reduce the problem to finding the limit of:

```
(1+1/n')^n'
```

as n' goes to infinity independently of the interest rate and the time interval.

You can investigate this quantity as n' gets bigger using a spreadsheet and you will find that it tends towards a value of 2.7182818285, which is known as the exponential number.

For example, in the spreadsheet below you can see a table of values of $(1+1/n')^{n'}$ for large, but certainly not infinite, values of n'. Notice how the value gets ever closer to the constant e. How far you can continue this process depends on the largest number that the spreadsheet you are using can cope with and on the accuracy of the calculation.

	A	B	C
	n'	(1+1/n')^n'	difference from e
1			
2	1	2	0.7182818284590
3	10	2.593742446	0.1245393683590
4	100	2.704813829	0.0134679990375
5	1000	2.716923932	0.0013578962235
6	10000	2.718145927	0.0001359016347
7	100000	2.718268237	0.0000135912615
8	1000000	2.718280469	0.0000013593026
9	10000000	2.718281694	0.0000001344787
10			

Given that the limit of $(1+1/n')^{n'}$ is e, the formula for the future value at any time t is simply:

```
FV=PV*e^(t*I)
```

The effect of continuous compounding is easily demonstrated in a chart.

To create a chart with $100 as the present value and 10% as the interest rate over a period of 40 years simply enter a series in column A from 0 to 40 years starting in A2, enter the formula:

```
=100*EXP(A2*0.1)
```

in B2 and copy it down the column to B42.

Then create an XY chart of the area A2:B42. Notice the characteristic way that the rate of increase is itself increasing.

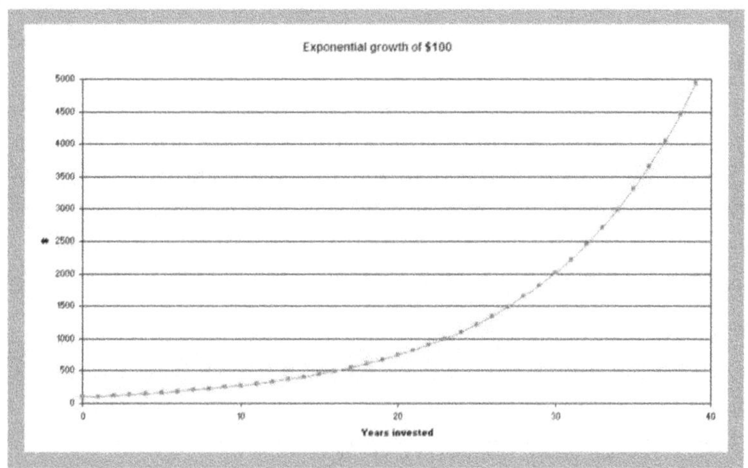

Once you have the formula for the Future Value working out the effective annual rate under continuous compounding is simple and gives:

```
effective rate = EXP(I)-1
```

Net and Gross - tax allowances

If interest is paid on a deposit then tax is usually payable on the income. Normally interest rates are quoted gross, i.e. without taking tax into account.

For example, if the deposit of $100 earns 10% effective per annum then $10 is earned in the first year, but T% of this has to be paid in tax, i.e. reducing it by T%.

Thus the interest actually received at the end of one year is:

```
tax paid interest=PV*I*(1-T)
```

You should be able to see that the effect of having to pay tax reduces the effective rate from I% to I*(1-T)%.

An interest rate that doesn't take tax into account is called a **gross** rate and one that does is called a **net** rate.

To convert from gross to net use the formula:

```
net = gross*(1-T)
```

To convert from net to gross use:

```
gross=net/(1-T)
```

For example, if a bank offers a gross rate of interest of 4% and tax is paid at 20%, then this is equivalent to receiving 0.04*(1-0.20) or 3.2% gross.

There is always the question of which rate should be quoted in connection with an interest bearing investment - gross nominal, net nominal, gross effective or net effective.

Financial institutions always prefer to quote the highest possible rate and this is, of course, the effective gross rate, also called the gross CAR (Compound Annual Rate). In all situations the net nominal rate should be converted to the net effective rate before being converted to the gross effective rate or gross CAR.

Of course what matters to the investor is the net effective rate because this reflects what is actually received on the investment. However, in comparing interest rates all that really matters is that the same type of rates are compared.

Calculating and compounding

There is one last complication to be considered. When a balance on deposit can vary from day-to-day calculating the interest to be added for a longer compounding period presents something of a problem.

For example, suppose a bank current account offers 1% per month with interest added monthly - what balance should be used to calculate the monthly interest?

As the balance can change each day it seems more reasonable to calculate the interest daily using a rate of I%/365 but only add the interest once a month.

This is how nearly all bank accounts work, including overdrafts, with interest calculated on the balance daily but only being added monthly or at a lesser frequency. (Of course the interest rate for an overdrawn account will be different from the one applied to one in credit.)

This doesn't alter any of the calculations described earlier and the effective rate is still given according to the compounding period and not according to period used to calculate the interest.

It is only when the interest is added to the account that matters. If the balance in the account is constant then the daily calculation of interest produces the same result as calculating and adding the interest at the end of each compounding period.

In the case of banks, the daily balance may not be what appears on the statement. The reason is that a check is credited to your account when it is paid in but only cleared for interest calculations three or so working days after that. The same is true of electronic transfers but with a shorter time before the balance is cleared.

Trying to keep an exact check on a daily bank balance can be very tricky as only the bank will actually know when a check or transfer has cleared for interest.

Examples

1) A bank's high interest check account offers interest calculated on the daily balance and added half yearly.

If the nominal gross interest rate is 8% per annum what is the effective rate?

The answer is that the compounding period is 6 monthly so the effective interest rate is simply

```
(1+0.08/2)^2-1
```

or 8.16%.

2) An account offers 8% on deposits calculated daily and paid annually.

What is the effective interest rate?

As the interest is added to the account annually there is no difference between the nominal and effective annual rates because there is no compounding. The danger here is to be misled into thinking that because the interest is calculated daily that it is compounded daily - it clearly isn't as it is only credited to the account once a year.

3) An even more complicated sounding interest arrangement is to be be found in the small print for an interest bearing current account:

> *" Interest is paid half yearly. It is calculated on a daily basis on cleared balances up to the first Friday in June and December and credited to your account on the third Friday."*

In fact it is just another example of interest calculated daily but added half yearly.

The reference to the first Friday and the third Friday simply make clear the lag between calculating the interest due and paying it. What the bank does is to calculate the interest due on the daily balance with a cut off point of the end of the first working week in June (and December). This amount is then added to the account on the third Friday of the same month.

Doesn't this mean that there is no interest being earned in the second week of the month?

No; the interest on the daily balance in the second week is part of the next six month's interest. The only disadvantage is that the interest calculated forgoes a week's interest before it is credited to the account and this lowers the effective interest rate, but not by enough to make it worth calculating.

4) The daily calculation of interest applies to bank accounts in overdraft as well as in credit. The rule is always that interest is charged or credited on the end of day balance. The rules for credit card debt are rather more complicated.

During the first month the amounts that you spend are added to give an end of month balance. This you must pay in part or in full within a fixed number of days of receiving your statement. Any balance that is outstanding after fixed number of days is up is charged interest daily starting from the date of each transaction. What this means is that if you pay within the fixed period then you can get free credit. But if you don't pay in full then you could have to pay interest from the time of purchase not just from the statement date.

The interest due on each purchase is simply:

```
Amount*Days*Interest*12/365
```

Notice the use of the factor 12/365 to convert a monthly interest rate to daily. This is a source of confusion as some companies will use a theoretical fixed length month to do the conversion. For example, if you assume that every month has 30 days the interest rate used is monthly interest/30 which is different from using 12/365 as the conversion factor.

Key points

- The effective or actual annual rate of interest gives the amount of interest earned per annum taking into account compounding. If the nominal annual rate is I then the effective annual rate is simply $(1+I)^n-1$ where n is the number of compounding periods per annum.

- The EIR/APR for a simple loan on which the interest is calculated periodically on the outstanding balance is just the effective annual rate (truncated to one decimal place in the UK). Notice that this is only true when no additional charges are made.

- If compounding occurs continuously then the effective rate is given by e^I-1.

- Tax reduces the amount that an investor actually receives. This can be summarized in terms of the net annual rate which is related to the gross rate by the formula, net = gross*(1-T)
where T is the tax rate.

- There are many situations in which interest is calculated and added at different periods so as to account for varying balances during the compounding period. All that matters from the point of view of calculating the effective rate is the compounding period.

Chapter 4

Introduction to Cashflow
Savings Plans

This is the first of three chapters covering the way in which interest rate affects cashflow. In it we explore savings, but first we introduce some general ideas that apply equally to annuities and repayment loans, which are covered in Chapters 5 and 6.

In the case of compound interest the value of the principal changes because of the interest added to it. This is just the simplest case of a regular alteration of the principal at the end of each compounding period. The next step is to include a regular payment or withdrawal. This is a remarkably common situation encountered in three major financial transactions repayment loans, savings plans and annuities.

Loans and annuities

In the case of a repayment loan or a mortgage (i.e. a repayment loan secured on property) the principal is reduced by the regular payment of the interest due plus an additional amount to pay off the loan. The repayments continue until the loan is paid off. Repayment loans are commonly encountered as part of Hire Purchase agreements for all types of goods and as repayment mortgages.

Although repayment loans are the most common example of this type of transaction every loan situation has its corresponding incarnation as an investment. Seen from the other side of the table, as it were, a repayment loan is called an annuity. In the case of an annuity a sum of money is placed on deposit and regular withdrawals composed of interest earned and capital are made. As in the case of a repayment loan the withdrawals continue until the deposit is reduced to zero. Annuities are most commonly encountered as part of a pension provision but they are applicable in any situation where an asset has to be converted into a regular cashflow.

As well as the lender/borrower view point there is also another variation on the repayment loan/annuity situation. In both the repayment loan and annuity the flow of cash acts to reduce the principal. In a regular savings plan the flow of cash acts to increase the principal. Apart from this change in direction of the cashflow the mathematics and many other consideration are identical.

Clearly the sorts of questions that interest us about repayment loans and annuities concern the size of the regular payment needed to reduce the principal to zero in a given number of years at the interest stated. As you might guess the formulas are the same for repayment loans and for annuities.

PV and FV

The basic idea is that there is a sum of money at the start of the process - the Present Value (PV). This is increased by the action of interest over time and either increased of decreased by a regular payment to give a sum of money in the future - the Future Value FV. We use the convention that the calculation is done from your point of view and money that you pay out is negative, i.e. it decreases your wealth.

In the case of a savings plan you initially deposit the present value (which is often zero) and make a regular payment each time period. As both of these are cashflows away from you, both are negative. Over time the action of interest and the regular payment increase the size of the deposit and hence its future value grows. Notice that the FV is positive because it is money you own.

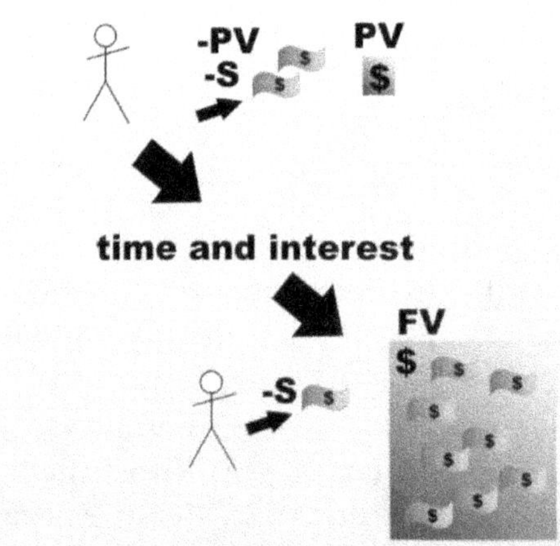

Savings plan - the deposit increases due to both payments and interest

The situation with an annuity is very similar. In this case the deposit i.e the PV starts out big and gets smaller as you withdraw money from it. Interest still acts to increase the deposit but usually the effect of the withdrawal slowly reduces the deposit to its future value which is usually taken to be zero.

In this case the cashflow in the first period is -PV representing the flow out of
the present value and +S representing the payment flowing in. In most cases
the FV, which is also positive in that it represents wealth you still hold, slowly
decreases, however this isn't always the case.

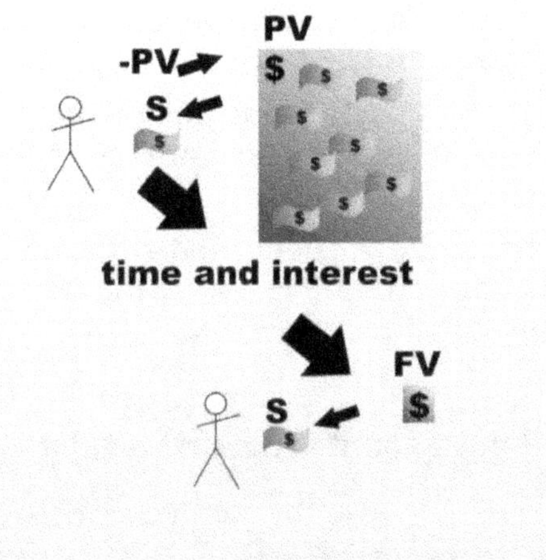

Annuity - the principal value is decreased by payments and increased by interest

Finally a repayment loan once again involves an initial sum, but in this case
the principal value is paid to you so it is positive. Your regular payment,
another negative cashflow, slowly reduces the debt. Notice that the future
value is negative as it represents a debt, i.e. a negative asset.

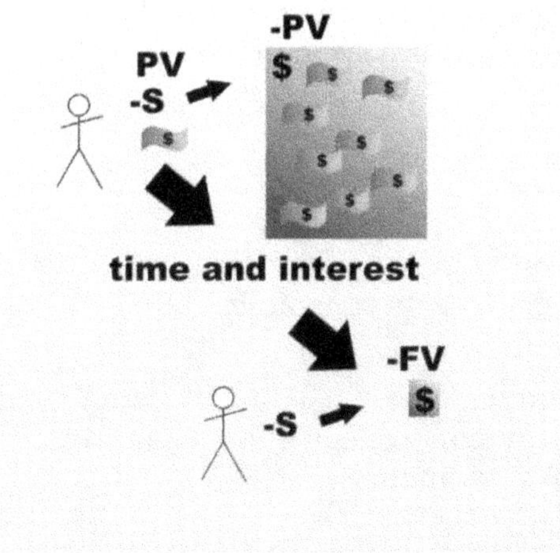

Repayment loan - the principal is slowly eroded by a cashflow

It has to be admitted that it is difficult to keep track of the signs of the cashflows, but if you apply the principle that a cashflow out is negative and a cashflow in is positive it should all work out.

Savings plans

The workings of a repayment loan or annuity are actually easier to understand if we first consider the closely related situation of a regular saving plan.

In this case a regular sum S (a payment, usually denoted PMT) is deposited each period and the total sum accumulated attracts interest at I% (Rate) at the end of each period.

It is a convention that the money is deposited at the end of each period and money that you pay out is negative. Thus after the first period the balance is simply the first regular payment:

```
= S
```

After the second period the amount is the first regular payment plus the interest it has earned:

```
=S*(1 + I) + S
```

After the third period the amount is:

```
=[S*(1 + I)+ S]*(1 + I) + S
```

and so on.

You can see that as each period passes the amount already on deposit is increased by being multiplied by (1+I) and has S added to it.

To work out the Future Value of the savings plan after n periods you could simply construct a spreadsheet that calculates the repeated multiplication by (1+I) and adding S but there is a simpler way of working out the same thing.

After a little math it can be shown that the Future Value is given by:

$$FV = S * \frac{(1 + I)^n - 1}{I}$$

This is such a complicated looking formula that nearly all spreadsheets provide a single financial function, usually called FV, to calculate the same result.

This is just the function we met in Chapter Two in the calculation of compound interest. Only now we can specify an initial deposit - the Present Value PV - and a regular payment S.

FV function

The common spreadsheet function:

```
=FV(I,NPER,S,PV)
```

will calculate the Future Value (FV) of a regular saving of S, at I% for nper periods with a starting balance of PV, which is often zero. If you don't specify the PV then it is assumed to be zero by default.

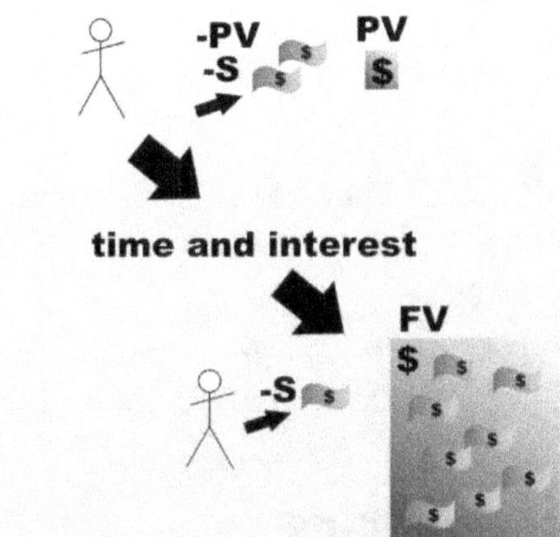

The cashflows are -PV and -S

Notice that as with nearly all financial functions it is best to regard the sums specified in the function, i.e. S and PV, as flowing from the depositor. So a deposit of $100 is -$100 and a payment of $10 per month into the account is -$10 per month. However the result of the function is the status of the account - positive when in credit and negative when in debt.

As with all financial calculations the interest rate has to be expressed in terms of the regular payment period and for a savings plan the money paid into the account is negative. For example, if you start a savings plan that calls for $10 per month at 6% per annum paid monthly then after 5 years the Future Value will be

```
=10*((1+0.06/12)^(5*12)-1)/(0.06/12)
```

```
=697.70
```

This is a horrible looking formula and one that you are very likely to make mistakes in when trying to enter it into a spreadsheet. How much simpler the equivalent financial functions appears:

```
=FV(0.06/12,5*12,-10)
```

and this of course gives exactly the same result, $697.70.

Notice that there is a minus sign in front of the payment reflecting the convention that cash paid in (e.g. S) is negative while cash paid out (e.g. FV) is positive.

If you make an initial deposit of PV at the start of the savings plan to get it going then the formula have to be altered to:

$$FV = S * \frac{(1 + I)^n - 1}{I} + PV*(1 + I)n$$

That is, the compounded interest earned by the initial deposit has to be added to the Future Value.

In most spreadsheets you simply include the initial deposit as the optional Present Value (PV) parameter at the end of the previous formula.

```
=FV(I,NPER,S,PV)
```

For example, if deposit $100 and save $10 per month at 6% per annum paid monthly then after 5 years the Future Value will be:

```
=FV(0.06/12,5*12,-10,-100)
```

which works out to $832.59. which is more than the previous result by $134.89 i.e. the amount of interest earned by the initial $100 at 6% for 5 years.

Ordinary and due annuities

You may be puzzled as to why in the calculation of the Future Value of the savings plan the first payment was made at the end of the first time period and so earned no interest.

The reason for adopting this convention is that it is used by nearly every spreadsheet's financial functions relating to annuities.

In fact there are two types of annuities:

- ordinary annuities where the payment is at the end of each period
- due annuities where payment is at the start of each period

In practice savings plans are usually calculated as due annuities so that when the plan has been running for n years it is indeed exactly n years since the first payment was made.

Nearly all spreadsheets include an optional **type** parameter as part of their financial functions that is set to zero to indicate that the payment is made at

the end of each period and one to indicate that the payment is made at the
end of the period. By default, i.e. if you omit the parameter as we have done
so far, then it is assumed that the payment is made at the end of each time
period.

At first the distinction between the two types of payment might seem
confusing but you can usually determine which you should use by asking
yourself a simple question.

Is there any interest involved in the first time period?

That is, if in month one you deposit $10 and the amount in the account at the
end of month one is $10 then no interest has been added. This is an ordinary
annuity and the formulas relating to it should have the type parameter set to
zero or omitted. If on the other hand the amount in the account at the end of
the first month is $10 plus the interest then we have a due annuity and the
type parameter should be set to one to calculate interest in the first period.

This sounds easy but it can still be confusing.

For example, if you open a savings plan that you have to pay in yearly it is
difficult to remember that the first payment represents the first year of an
ordinary annuity and attracts no interest.

So, if you pay $100 per year at 10% per annum into a savings plan then the
standard FV formula gives that at the end of the first year you have :

```
=FV(10%,1,-100)
```

which works out to $100. By default an ordinary annuity has been calculated
where the payment is at the end of the first time period and so no interest is
due.

However, for a savings plan you would expect to earn interest in the first year
and so the correct formula is with the type parameter set to one:

```
=FV(10%,1,-100,0,1)
```

Notice that we now have to specify PV as zero because we need to specify the
last parameter to the function and hence need to enter some value for the one
before. In this case the formula returns the result $110 to indicate that the
payment was made at the start of the period and so earned interest.

There is also a the potential to confuse the role of any lump sum that starts a
savings plan. The initial deposit is assumed to earn interest during the first
period in both types of annuity calculation.

That is, if you start the savings plan used above with an initial deposit of $100
then the ordinary annuity calculation gives for the first year:

```
=FV(10%,1,-100,-100,0)
```

which works out to $210 i.e. the initial $100 made $10 interest plus the
payment of $100 at the end of the year which did not make any interest.

For a due annuity the calculation is:

```
=FV(10%,1,-100,-100,1)
```

which works out to $220 because the initial $100 made $10 interest and the first payment made at the start of the year also made $10 interest giving $220. In most cases you can work out which type of calculation you need to do by considering the situation at the end of the first time period. Notice that most of the financial functions concerned with periodic payments have a final type parameter that works in more or less the same way.

Payment

Once we have a formula that gives the Future Value given the interest rate and the term, the next obvious question is what the corresponding formulas are for the interest rate given the Future value and the term; and for the term given the interest rate and the Future Value.

If you want to save an amount of money equal to FV in n time periods with interest rate I, you have to save:

$$S = \frac{FV*I}{(1 + I)^n - 1}$$

per time period.

As you might expect for such a complicated formula most spreadsheets have an equivalent financial function PMT:

```
S=PMT(I,n,PV,FV,type)
```

where I is the interest rate, n the number of periods, PV the initial deposit i.e. the Present Value and FV the final or Future Value of the account. The final parameter type is zero or one depending on whether the payments are at the start or end of each time period. If the savings scheme starts from a zero balance then the present value PV is zero.

For example, if you want to save for a final sum of $697.7 in 5 years at an interest rate of 6% per annum paid monthly then you would use:

```
=PMT(0.06/12,5*12,0,697.7)
```

which returns a result of -$10 per month which agrees with the previous example.

The FV is regarded as positive because it is the value of the account in 5 years time. Notice that the payment is negative indicating that you have to pay into the savings scheme. You can, of course, include an initial sum in the saving scheme and specify if the payments are to be at the start or the end of each period.

For example, suppose that we have an initial deposit of $100 then the at the same interest rate over five years you need to deposit:

`=PMT(0.06/12,5*12,-100,697.7)`

which works out to only -$8.07 per month.

Notice that the PV is a negative cashflow. If you make a mistake and enter a positive PV then you should spot the error by noticing that the monthly payment goes up!

Number of periods (NPER)

Similarly if you want to know how long you will have to wait before a savings plan produces a given sum i.e. the FV then you have to work out:

```
            FV*I
     ln(1+ -----)
             S
n = ------------
      ln(1+I)
```

This too is a horrible looking formula and so there is corresponding financial function:

`n=NPER(I,S,PV,FV,type)`

Once again I is the interest rate, S the periodic sum, PV the Present value, which can be zero, and FV the Future Value. The final parameter type is zero or one depending on whether the payments are at the start or end of each time period.

For example, if you want to save for a final sum of $697.7 at an interest rate of 6% per annum paid monthly and you can save $10 per month then then you would use:

`=NPER(0.06/12,-10,0,697.7)`

which returns a result of 59.999 months which agrees with the previous example i.e. roughly 5 years.

Notice that in this case it is vital that you get the sign on the payment correct. If you enter a positive value then this means that the savings plan pay you $10 at the end of each month and to reach the final FV you would have to "save" for -86 months. A result that is mostly nonsense!

You can, of course, include an initial sum in the saving scheme and specify if the payments are to be at the start or the end of each period.

Interest rate (RATE)

Now we come to the interesting calculation of the interest needed to make a regular payment of S grow to FV in n periods. This problem has no easy solution.

There literally is no way of juggling the values in the formula to solve for I. The best we can do is make a guess at I and see if the value of FV computed using it is too high or too low. Using this information a new guess can be made that is closer to the correct value. The process is repeated until the guessed value of I is close enough to the value that we are looking for.

This guessing process is generally called 'iteration' and some spreadsheets do provide a financial function that will solve for I.

Most spreadsheets have a RATE function which can be used to find the interest rate for a savings plan as

```
I= RATE(n,S,PV,FV,type,guess)
```

where n is the number of periods, S the payment, PV the inital balance, FV the final balance, type is zero or one depending on whether the payments are the start or the end of the time periods and guess is a guess at what the interest rate is. If you don't specify a guess then a random value is used as the starting value.

For example, if you want to accumulate $697.7 by saving $10 per month for five years you would need to find an interest rate of:

```
=RATE(5*12,-10,0,697.7)*12
```

which is 6% per annum paid monthly. Notice the need to multiply by 12 to convert the monthly rate to a per annum rate.

The question remains what should be done in the case of a spreadsheet that doesn't have a financial function to calculate I?

The solution is to implement the iterative method directly. Using standard techniques (Newton's method) it is relatively easy to work out that if I is a guess at the interest rate then

$$I_{new} = I - \frac{S*(I_{old})^{n-1} - FV*I}{S*n*(1+I_{old})^{n-1} - FV}$$

is closer to the true value.

This is another horrible looking formula, but once entered into a spreadsheet it can be worked out without effort. The big difference is that it has to be worked out more than once to repeatedly improve the guess until it is close enough to the true value to make no practical difference. Each time the new I obtained from the use of the formula is fed back into the equation to give another new value of I and so on until the change in the value with each iteration is very small. This may sound very complicated but in fact it is very easy to incorporate into a spreadsheet.

Savings plan calculator

Using the formulas derived in the previous section it is fairly simple to create a savings plan calculator that will supply the missing value given any three of FV, S, I and n.

First enter the spreadsheet title and the row and column headings shown below:

	A	B	C	D	E	F
1	Monthly Savings Plan	(Payments at the start of each month)				
2						
3						
4		Future	Interest	Payment	Term	
5		Value	Rate			
6	Future Value	£14,720.58	£14,720.58	£14,720.58	£14,720.58	
7	Interest Rate (per annum)	8%	8%	8%	8%	
8	Payment (per month)	25	25	24.83	25	
9	Term (years)	20	20	20	19.9302854	
10						

The actual work of calculation is done by the formulas along the diagonal in the shaded cells. Each formula calculates one of FV, I, S and n as indicated by the headings.

The relevant formulas that you need to enter are:

```
=FV(B7/12,B9*12,-B8,1) in B6
```

```
=RATE(C9*12,-C8,0,C6,1)*12 in C7
```

```
=-PMT(D7/12,D9*12,0,D6,1) in D8
```

```
=NPER(E7/12,-E8,0,E6,1)/12 in E9
```

Now if you enter values into the other cells, these formulas work out the remaining values.

The type parameter is set to 1 in each case because you usually want to calculate a savings plan so that the payments are at the start of each time period.

Notice that the use of negative signs to indicate which values are paid out from the user. The PMT function automatically gives the correct answer as a negative value but as all of the other payments in the row have been entered using the convention that payments are positive a minus sign is added.

Also notice that the NPER function automatically returns the answer in months but the spreadsheet is working in years - hence the division by 12 - and the Rate function returns a monthly interest rate - hence the need to multiply by 12 to give a per annum rate.

Generally it's the attention to detail such as signs and units of time that makes a financial spreadsheet trickier than you might initially think!.

Formula summary

The following formulas were introduced in this chapter:

FV balance	`FV(I,n,S,PV,type)`
S payment	`PMT(I,n,PV,FV,type)`
n number of periods	`NPER(I,S,PV,FV,type)`
I interest rate	`RATE(n,S,PC,FV,type,guess)`

For a savings plan, type is usually set to 1 and PV is often 0.

Chapter 5

Cashflow Continued
Annuities

Although a savings plan is just a special case of an annuity, it has become common practice to apply the term to a particular type of investment where a lump sum is exchanged for a cashflow, whereas with a savings plan where a cashflow is exchanged for a lump sum. In the case of an annuity the cashflow reduces the principal but interest still acts to increase it.

Annuities explored

In the case of an annuity the regular payment positive (i.e. a cash inflow) and the initial deposit negative (i.e. a cash outflow). The cashflow reduces the principal but interest still acts to increase it

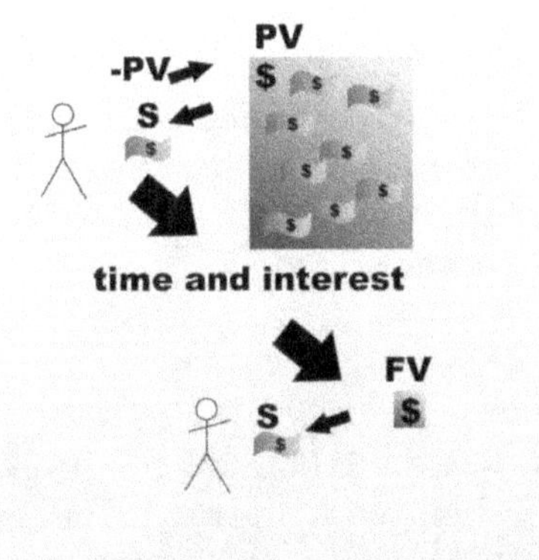

An annuity - the deposit decreases as cash is withdrawn, but interest acts to increase it

If the amount deposited is PV and the amount periodically withdrawn is S (which is positive as it represents cash flowing to you) then at the end of the first time period the balance stands at:

```
PV*(1 + I)-S
```

At the end of the second:

```
(PV*(1 + I)-S)*(1 + I)-S = PV*(1 + I)*(1 + I)- S*(1 + I)- S
```

and so on.

Each month the balance earns I% interest and so increases by (1+I) but then S is removed from the account.

In general after n time periods the balance stands at:

```
PV*(1 + I)^n − S*(1 + I)^(n-1)- S*(1 + I) ...-S
```

We already have a formula that gives the future value, i.e. the balance at time n, and it is just the formula used for the savings plan when there is an initial deposit PV :

$$FV = \frac{S*(1+I)^n}{I} + PV*(1+I)^n$$

and as long as we regard the cashflow as positive and the initial deposit as negative (i.e. money you paid out) then we don't even have to change the sign of S in the formula.

That is, the function:

```
=FV(I,NPER,S,PV)
```

will calculate the Future Value FV of an annuity consisting of a regular payment of S, at I% for nper periods with a starting balance of PV. (Note that in Excel's terminology PMT is used for S and Rate for I.)

In the case of an annuity PV is usually negative and the payment S is positive. For example, suppose we set up an annuity with a PV of -$1000, then at an interest rate of 10% per annum if we withdraw $100 each year the FV or balance at the end of one year is:

```
=FV(10%,1,200,-1000)
```

which gives $900.

The reason is that the interest on $1000 is $100, making the balance at the end of the year $1100 and then we withdraw $200, reducing the balance to $ 900.

The following year the balance will be:

```
=FV(10%,2,200,-1000)
```

which works out to $790 - i.e. plus $90 of interest and minus the $200 withdrawal and so on.

Number of periods to zero

The FV function can be used to give the balance after any number of periods but what usually interests us is when the balance will be reduced to zero. The reason is that when the balance is reduced to zero the cashflow stops and thus this is the lifetime of the annuity. We can also ask other obvious questions, such as given a sum of money and an interest rate how much can be withdrawn, given the cashflow has to last n time periods.

The first formula that we need is the number of periods it takes to reduce the Future Value to 0:

$$FV = -S\frac{(1+I)^n}{I} + PV*(1+I)^n = 0$$

Solving this equation for n gives:

$$n = \frac{-\ln\left(1 - \dfrac{PV*I}{S}\right)}{\ln(1+I)}$$

If this looks like an unappealing formula then you will be pleased to know that most spreadsheets supply a suitable financial function to make it unnecessary to struggle with the real thing.

To calculate the number of periods needed to reduce the Future Value of an annuity to zero you can use the NPER function that has already been introduced but this time with the FV set to zero:

```
n = NPER(I,S,PV,0,type)
```

For example, how long will an annuity paying $200 with an interest rate of 10% and an initial deposit of $1000 take to exhaust the capital? The answer is:

```
=NPER(10%,200,-1000,0)
```

which works out to approximately 7.27 years.

If you use the FV function to work out the balance after 7 years:

```
=FV(10%,7,200,-1000)
```

you will discover that there is only just over $51 left in the account - not enough to pay the annuity in the following year.

If this is a guaranteed annuity, i.e. one that is paid until the holder dies, then this is the point at which the annuity provider starts to make a loss.

You can also see that with a table that gives the probability of dying, an actuarial table, you can easily work out the expected return on a guaranteed annuity.

Present Value

You can find the Present Value, i.e. the amount needed to be deposited to provide a payment S for n periods with interest rate I, of regular payments, using the formula:

$$PV = S \frac{1-(1+I)^n}{I}$$

Most spreadsheets provide a financial function to find PV:

```
=PV(I,n,S,FV,type)
```

This gives the amount needed to generate a payment of S for n periods given an interest rate of I, leaving FV in the account at the end of n periods. Usually FV is set to zero because you need to know the minimum amount needed to fund the cashflow without leaving a residual sum in the account. For example, if you need a cashflow of $200 per month for 7 years at 10% per annum then the amount you need to deposit is:

```
=PV(10%,7,200,0)
```

This works out to -937.68, which is a little less than the 1000 in the previous examples.

Calculating Payments

Finding the regular amount that can be taken given the value of the annuity and the interest rate produces a fairly simple looking formula:

$$S = \frac{PV * I}{1-(1+I)^n}$$

Nearly all spreadsheets have a simple financial function that will work out such payments. Usually it is PMT, the same one that works out the payments for a savings plan:

```
S=PMT(Rate,NPER,PV,FV,type)
```

where Rate is the interest rate (which is normally denoted I in this book), nper the number of periods, PV (Present Value) is the initial deposit and FV (Future Value) is the final sum of money in the account.

For example, how much can you take for 7 years if the initial deposit is $1000 and the interest rate is 10% per annum:

```
=PMT(10%,7,-1000,0)
```

This works out to $205.41, which again should be compared to the result given earlier that taking $200 leaves a little in the account after 7 years. This payment reduces the account to exactly zero after exactly 7 years.

Interest by iteration

Once again, as in the case of the savings plan, solving for I turns out to be impossible and iteration has to be used. In most cases you can find the interest rating using the function:

```
=RATE(NPER,PMT,PV,FV,type,guess)
```

For example, if you take $200 for 7 years from an initial deposit of $1000 what interest rate to you need to make the final balance zero:

```
=RATE(7,200,-1000,0)
```

which works out to 9% per annum.

An annuity calculator

Now that we have the formulas to calculate any one of PV, I, S and n given values for the other three it is quite easy to construct an annuity calculator spreadsheet along the same lines as the savings plan calculator given in Chapter 4.

	A	B	C	D	E	F
1	Annuity	(Payments at the end of each time period)				
2						
3						
4		Present	Interest	Payment	Term	
5		Value	Rate			
6	Present Value	2,988.86	2,988.86	2,988.86	2,988.86	
7	Interest Rate (per annum)	8%	8%	8%	8%	
8	Payment (per month)	25	25	25.00	25	
9	Term (years)	20	20	20	20	
10						

The annuity calculator

Set up the spreadsheet shown above with a 4 by 4 grid for Present Value, Interest Rate, Payment and Term, entering the following formulas into the cells along the diagonal:

```
=PV(B7/12,B9*12,-B8) in B6
=RATE(C9*12,C8,-C6,0)*12 in C7
=PMT(D7/12,D9*12,-D6,0) in D8
=NPER(E7/12,E8,-E6,0)/12 in E9
```

When you enter three known values into the other cells in the grid, these formulas will calculate the remaining one in these calls. Here we use the same values to show that it works.

Formula summary

The formulas introduced in Chapter 4 were used again in this chapter:

FV balance	`FV(I,n,S,PV,type)`
S payment	`PMT(I,n,PV,FV,type)`
n number of periods	`NPER(I,S,PV,FV,type)`
I interest rate	`RATE(n,S,PC,FV,type,guess)`

For an ordinary annuity, type is set to 0 or omitted and FV is often 0.

Chapter 6

Exploring Repayment Loans

A repayment loan is particularly easy to deal with because it is just an annuity seen from a different point of view.

In the case of a repayment loan a sum of money - the principal or Present Value PV is borrowed at the start of the loan. At the end of each time period a regular sum S is paid back. This regular sum has to be large enough to pay back the interest due on the loan and some of the principal. As long as this is the case the proportion of interest to principal repaid each period changes so that more and more of the principal is repaid. Eventually the entire principal is repaid and the debt is cleared.

A repayment loan may be just an annuity seen from the other side of the table but the sort of questions you need to answer are subtly different. Partly this is due to a slight difference in psychology and the nature of the decisions you have to make. You are trying to minimize the interest rate and term rather than maximize them - but it is also the way that institutions and the law deal differently with loans than annuities.

In a repayment loan what interests us most is the size of the repayment given the loan, interest and term but there are still lots of reasons to need to calculate any of the four quantities - repayment, interest rate, term and loan amount - given the remaining three.

Turning the tables

The basic mathematics of repayment loans is the same as for an annuity. At the start of the loan the amount PV is borrowed - this is a cashflow in and so positive, however the balance in the account at this point is negative to signify a debt.

At the end of the first period the debt has increased to:

```
PV*(1+I)
```

but the payment of S has also reduced it. That is, at the end of the first period the balance stands at:

```
PV*(1+I)-S
```

At the end of the second period the balance stands at:

```
[PV*(1+I)-S]*(1+I)-S = PV*(1+I)*(1+I)-S*(1+I)-S
```

and so on.

In general after *n* time periods the balance stands at

```
PV*(1+I)^n - S*(1+I)^(n-1)- S*(1+I) ...-S
```

which is of course the same as the situation encountered in the case of the ordinary annuity. Thus all of the equations, and even the spreadsheets. that we have constructed for the ordinary annuity apply to the repayment loan.

The only difference is that now the Present Value (PV) is the amount loaned and the payments are to repay the debt. After all one man's annuity investment is another's repayment loan.

In more practical terms this means that in terms of the cashflows the present value is positive because it is what the borrower receives, i.e. cash in, and the regular payments are negative, i.e. cash out. One final possible confusion is that the financial functions return a negative value of the PV or FV because it represents a debt.

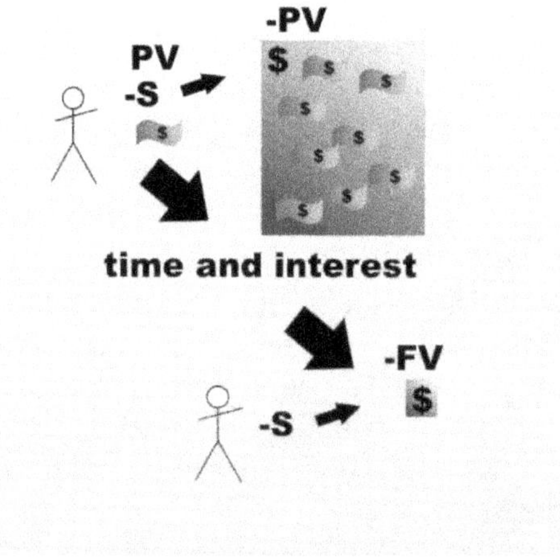

Cashflow in a loan

The function:

```
=FV(I,nper,S,PV,type)
```

will calculate the Future Value FV of a repayment loan of PV being paid back at a rate of S per time period with interest at I%. As already explained **type** is 0 if the payment is at the start of the period and 1 if it is at the end.

For a repayment loan the payment is at the start of the period and isn't involved in the interest rate calculation until the following period. Also PV is positive and S (PMT in Excel's terminology) is negative.

In other words if you borrow PV at an interest rate of I% per period and pay the loan back at S per period then FV is the state of the account i.e. the debt after nper periods.

For example, if you borrow $1000 at 15% per annum paid annually then if you repay $200 per year after the first year the account stands at:

```
=FV(15%,1,-200,1000)
```

or -$950 i.e. the debt has reduced by $150. After 1 year the debt has increased to -$1150 and you have repaid $200 making a total of -$950 as given. In 10 years the debt is reduced to

```
=FV(15%,10,-200,1000)
```

which works out to $15.19 and a positive value indicates that the loan has been over paid by this amount - i.e. the loan was fully repaid sometime during the 10th year.

Number of periods to repay the loan

The FV function can be used to give the balance after any number of periods but it is also important to know when the loan is repaid - i.e. when the FV becomes zero.

To calculate the number of periods needed to reduce the Future Value to zero you can use the NPER function that has already been introduced in earlier chapters but this time with the FV set to zero:

```
n = NPER(I,S,PV,0,type)
```

For example, how long will it take to repay a loan of $1000 at 15% at a rate of $200 per year? The answer is:

```
=NPER(15%,-200,1000,0)
```

which works out to approximately 9.92 years. This agrees with the earlier calculation that the same loan is repaid before 10 years are up.

Present value of a loan

In the case of a repayment loan the present value represents the amount that can be borrowed if you can find a loan at a given rate, term and payment. We use the PV function that has been introduced in earlier chapters, but with FV, the target value at the end of the term, generally set to zero:

```
=PV(I,n,S,0,type)
```

gives the amount you can borrow if the interest rate is I and the loan is repaid with n periodic payments of S.

For example, if you can pay $200 per month for 10 years at 15% per annum, you can borrow:

`=PV(15%,10,-200,0)`

which works out to $1003.75, a little more than the $1000 in the previous examples.

Calculating repayments

Another important repayment calculation is the amount needs to be paid to clear a loan at a given rate and term. As repayment loans are generally arrange on the basis of the amount for a given term this is particularly important. This is achieved using the PMT function, again with FV set to 0:

`S = PMT(I,n,PV,0,type)`

where I is the interest rate, n the number of periods, PV the size of the loan.

For example, how much do you have to pay to repay a loan of $1000 at 15% in exactly 10 years?

The formula needed is:

`=PMT(15%,10,1000,0)`

which works out to -$199.25, which again should be compared to the result given earlier.

A far less common calculation for a repayment loan is to find the interest rate needed to repay the loan in a given time at a given rate. The reason is simply that usually you are in search of the lowest rate available not the one that fits the time period and repayments exactly. However the calculation is worth exploring for completeness and just in case it is needed as a way of judging the value of a given financial arrangement in terms of the equivalent repayment loan rate.

Once again, as in the case of the savings plan, solving for I turns out to be impossible and iteration has to be used. In most cases you can simply use the RATE function with FV set to zero:

`I= RATE(n,S,PV,0,type,guess)`

where n is the number of periods, S the payment, PV the loan, type is zero or one depending on whether the payments are the start or the end of the time periods and guess is a guess at what the interest rate is. If you don't specify a guess then a random value is used as the starting value.

For example, what rate do you need to completely repay a loan of $1000 over 10 years of repaying $100 per year?

The formula you need is:

```
=RATE(10,-200,1000,0)
```

which works out to 15% per annum, a value that again should be compared to the previous examples.

Repayment schedules

Repayment loans are often arranged and then subject to much on-going scrutiny and possible rearrangement in the light of new financial circumstances. As a result the detailed workings of change in the debt and where the payments are going are usually of concern. The same calculations apply both to annuities and savings plans with minor modifications.

As well as knowing the values relating to the end of the loan or annuity it is also often necessary to know the balance at any time. This is just the future value at the specified time. That is, the balance of a loan of PV at I% repaid at S per period after n periods is:

```
=FV(I,n,S,PV)
```

For example, a loan of $1000 at 15% repaid at $200 per annum has a balance after 6 years of:

```
=FV(15%,6,-200,1000)
```

which is -$562.31.

As well as knowing the balance you might also want to know the amount of the principal that has been repaid. This is simply the difference between the PV and the balance, i.e. the reduction in the debt:

```
=PV-FV(I,n,S,PV)
```

For example, after 6 years of a loan of $1000 at 15% repaid at $200 per annum the amount of the loan repaid is:

```
=-1000-FV(15%,6,-200,1000)
```

which works out to -$437.69.

In the same way the amount of interest paid to date is easily found as the difference between the total amount paid and the amount of the loan repaid :

```
=n*S-PV+FV(I,n,S,PV)
```

For example, after 6 years of a loan of $1000 at 15% repaid at $200 per annum the amount paid in interest is:

```
=-6*200+1000+FV(15%,6,-200,1000)
```

which works out to -$762.31.

There are a range of spreadsheet functions that will give you the amount of the loan and the interest repaid in any given time period, but it is generally easier to use the basic functions we have already met.

All of the functions given above work out a cumulative total for the amount repaid and for interest. You can use these to find the amount in any given period, n say, simply by taking the difference between the cumulative amount at time n-1 and at n.

For example: the amount of the debt repaid in time period n is just the difference between FV at period n-1 and period n:

`=FV(I,n-1,S,PV)-FV(I,n,S,PV)`

and the amount paid in interest in period n is just the difference in cumulative interest between period n-1 and n:

`=(n-1)*S-PV + FV(I,n-1,S,PV)- n*S + PV + FV(I,n,S,PV)`

which after a little algebra reduces to:

`=FV(I,n-1,S,PV)-FV(I,n,S,PV)-S`

You should see that this is just the difference between the payment and the amount paid off the debt in that period. This is exactly what you would expect as each payment goes in part to pay off the loan amount and part to pay the interest.

Formula summary

FV balance	`=FV(I,n,S,PV,type)`
S payment	`=PMT(I,n,PV,0,type)`
n number of periods	`=NPER(I,S,PV,0,type)`
I interest rate	`=RATE(n,S,PV,0,type,guess)`
Total repaid at n	`=PV-FV(I,n,S,PV)`
Total interest at n	`=n*S-PV+FV(I,n,S,PV)`

For a repayment loan type is set to zero or omitted and FV is zero.

Loan schedule calculator

Using these formulas it is quite easy to put together a spreadsheet that will detail the state of a repayment loan at any stage in its life. The only real problem is allowing for the required number of months in the table.

First enter all of the text and Loan, Rate and Term data as shown in the screen dump.

Enter 1 in A8 to start the formula off and enter:

```
=FV($B$2/12,A8*12,$B$5, $B$1) in B8
```

```
=$B$5*A8*12 in C8
```

```
=$B$1+B8 in D8
```

```
=-(C8-D8) in E8
```

The first formula computes the state of the account at the end of each year. The second works out the total amount paid by the end of the year and the final two work out the amount of the debt paid off and the amount paid in interest to date.

Next fill column A with as many year numbers as you are interested in and copy the formulas in B8:G8 into the same number of rows.

You can see an example of a 25-year loan in the spreadsheet. Notice the way that the first year's payments only succeed in paying off $21.02 of the principal even though over $4400 is paid! Over the 25-year period of the loan more than $130,000 is paid in interest.

	A	B	C	D	E
1	Loan	20000			
2	Rate	22%	per annum paid monthly		
3	Term	25	years		
4					
5	Payment	-368.25			
6					
7	Year	Balance	Total Paid	Debt paid	Interest paid
8	1	-19978.98	-4418.98	21.02	4440.00
9	2	-19952.85	-8837.96	47.15	8885.12
10	3	-19920.34	-13256.94	79.66	13336.60
11	4	-19879.92	-17675.93	120.08	17796.01
12	5	-19829.65	-22094.91	170.35	22265.26
13	6	-19767.13	-26513.89	232.87	26746.76
14	7	-19689.39	-30932.87	310.61	31243.48
15	8	-19592.71	-35351.85	407.29	35759.14
16	9	-19472.48	-39770.83	527.52	40298.36
17	10	-19322.96	-44189.82	677.04	44866.86
18	11	-19137.02	-48608.80	862.98	49471.78
19	12	-18905.78	-53027.78	1094.22	54122.00
20	13	-18618.22	-57446.76	1381.78	58828.55
21	14	-18260.60	-61865.74	1739.40	63605.14
22	15	-17815.87	-66284.72	2184.13	68468.85

Loan schedule calculator

Loan balance reduction over time

The way in which loan repayments affect the amount you owe is much easier
to appreciate in a chart which can be constructed directly from this
spreadsheet with Year (Column A) on the x-axis and Balance (Column B) on
the y-axis.

If you look at the graph of the balance against time you can see the
characteristic shape of the repayment loan. The principal is paid off only
slowly at first but the speed of repayment increases dramatically in the final
years.

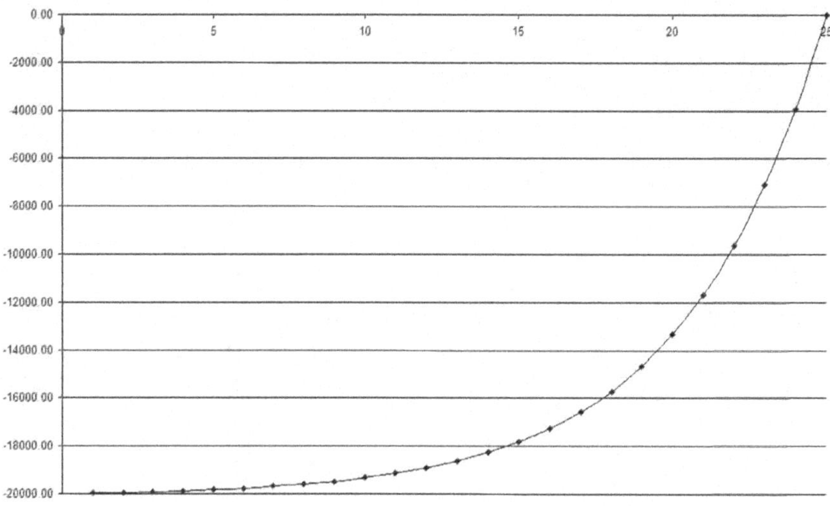

The rate of decrease of a repayment loan

Notice that there is no real decrease in the amount owed for the first 15 years.
This is the reason why additional payments early in the life of a loan can
greatly reduce the total cost.

Chapter 7

Coping With Irregular Cashflow

In earlier chapters we have examined how money behaves under some particularly simple situations - a single deposit or loan accruing interest and the effect of a regular cashflow on the same. In real life cashflows are often irregular, both in time and in amount. This makes it difficult to evaluate the worth of an investment or the cost of a loan that involves irregular payments. However all is not lost because there are a range of methods that can be used to compare such investments and loans.

In this and the next chapter we examine the ideas of the present and future value of money and see how these ideas can be used to make judgments about the worth of an investment.

Time value of money

The most important thing to realize when evaluating an investment is that money now is worth more than money in the future, even if you ignore the action of inflation.

The reason is that money that you have now can be invested and can earn a safe rate of interest. If you are deprived of a sum of money until a later date then you have to take into account the loss of interest. You can think of this as an opportunity cost of not having the money.

If the prevailing 'no risk' interest rate is I% then \$PV will grow to \$FV given by:

```
FV = PV*(1+I)^n
```

in n time periods.

The present value grows into the future value by the action of compound interest. This relationship can be turned the other way about and we can say that the future value can be discounted back to its equivalent present value.

This relationship between Future Value and Present Value is fundamental to the measurement of the time value of money.

If you are to receive a sum of money in the future then what ever it is worth then it is only worth the equivalent present value now.

That is, all Future Values should be reduced to their corresponding Present Values before their worth can be assessed using:

```
PV = FV/(1+I)^n
```

You can think of this as reducing future sums of money by a discount factor to allow for the effect of interest.

For example, if you are to receive $100 in 5 years time, i.e. FV=500 and n=5*12, the Present Value is given by:

```
PV = 500/(1+0.08/12)^(5*12) = 355.60
```

So if you were offered $500 in 5 years time or $355.60 now there would be no reason to prefer one or the other on purely financial grounds.

It is in this sense that the present value and the future value represent the same amount of wealth; one will become the other by the action of time and interest.

Safe interest rate

Of course the equivalence of FV and PV does depend on the interest rate that you choose to use in the formula and this adds a degree of arbitrariness into the comparison. In practice you should use an interest rate that makes the comparison meaningful to you. For example, there is no point in using an interest rate that is not accessible to you or to the sum of money under consideration. So using a high rate that can only be obtained by large deposits isn't reasonable in most cases, neither is a high risk rate. You should in general choose an interest rate that is readily obtainable and regarded as a safe investment.

There is another problem in that safe interest rates may vary over the period of the calculation and so alter the present value. However, factors that alter the 'safe' interest rate also tend to affect the return on every type of investment and so the alter the future value in the same way as the present value. As a result the present value still provides an excellent way of comparing different investment opportunities.

Interest rates and inflation

The effect of inflation on interest rates and investments is a very general concern and it could be discussed in almost any chapter of this book. However it is particularly relevant to a discussion of the time value of money.

If we are discounting future cash amounts to allow for the 'natural' growth in money due to the availability of a safe interest rate, then why not also discount to adjust for inflation?

This is a perfectly reasonable procedure and something that can be done quite easily if you have an estimate of the inflation rate. If you receive $F n years in the future then its deflated value now is simply:

`P=F/(1-R)^n`

where R is the effective annual inflation rate. Notice that this calculation has nothing at all to do with the mechanism by which the future sum of money is acquired. It could be the promised cash lump sum received as part of a pension, or the accumulated growth of an investment.

The calculation of the deflated value is identical in form to the calculation of the present value. This raises the question of how the two are related and whether or not we should also deflate as well as discount the future value?

The deflated value takes account of the loss of purchasing power of money. That is, having $F in the future will allow you to buy the same goods as having $P today would do. The present value, on the other hand, does not take into account the purchasing power of money, only the lost investment revenue due to not receiving money for n years.

The point is that inflation does not directly alter the amount of money that you need to invest now to receive another sum in n years time. In this sense inflation does not affect the concept or method of calculation of the present value nor the relationship between present and future value.

In general:

- the present value of a future cash sum is not affected by inflation even though the purchasing power of the future value is.

True rate

It is worth pointing out that there is a generally accepted connection between inflation and the prevailing safe interest rate.

Many investors are familiar with the notion of the 'true' interest rate, which roughly means an interest rate adjusted for inflation. For example, if you are offered an interest rate of 8% and inflation is running at 3% then the 'true' interest rate is approximately only 8 - 3% i.e. 5%. What this means is that the purchasing power of this investment is growing at a rate of 5% and not 8% per annum.

As was explained in chapter 1 simply subtracting the inflation rate from the interest to give the true interest rate is a useful rough and ready approximation but it isn't quite accurate. If inflation is running at R% per annum and the investment is made at I% per annum then each year the purchasing power of the deposit $M decreases by (1-R) and the amount on deposit increases by (1+I). Thus each year the overall change in purchasing power of the investment is:

`=M*(1 + I)(1-R)`

If i is the 'true' interest rate, then the purchasing power of the deposit is given by

=M*(1 + i)

You can see from these two formulas that

(1 + i) = (1 + I)(1 - R)

If you multiply out the right-hand side you get

1 + i = 1 + I − R − I*R

or

i=I-R-I*R

In other words, the true interest rate is worked out by subtracting the inflation rate and subtracting IR. For example, in the case of 8% interest and 3% inflation the true interest rate is (0.08-0.03 -0.08*0.03)=0.0476 or 4.8%.

As you can see the additional -I*R usually makes only a small difference and you can safely carry on using the 'interest minus inflation' rule to estimate the true interest rate unless interest or inflation makes I*R big enough to worry about.

Of course the need to subtract I*R to get the accurate true rate is also the reason why you need more than R% interest to compensate for inflation. For example, if the interest rate is 6% and inflation is also 6% the true rate of interest is -0.06*0.06 or -0.36%.

You can make use of the true interest rate to work out the increase in the purchasing power of an investment by simply using the true rate in place of the interest rate in any of the calculations described earlier.

For example, if you make a single investment of $1000 at an annual interest rate of 8% for 10 years then the final balance will be:

=1000*(1+0.08)^10 =$2158.92

However, if inflation is running at 5% per annum the true interest rate is only 2.6%, making the final balance only worth:

=1000*(1+0.026)^10 =$1292.63

in the prevailing terms.

You can arrive at similar inflation adjusted estimates by using the true interest rate in place of the quoted interest rate.

In the case of a loan the estimate of the true interest is usually sufficient in itself. For example, if a mortgage is offered at 8% per annum and inflation is running at 4% then the true interest rate is only 3.68%. Clearly in times of high inflation it is possible for the true rate to be negative.

Notice that the calculation of the true interest rate assumes no underlying theory of how interest rates are set. It is a purely arithmetic relationship between the action of inflation and interest. However, it seems a reasonable assumption that the quoted interest rate should reflect the estimated inflation rate. That is, the true rate of interest is determined by the real growth in wealth and then the quoted rate is 'adjusted' by inflation. Even if this theory does not apply and the true interest rate is not a fundamental economic quantity this makes no difference to the fact that it does at least measure the real increase in wealth.

Net present value

The idea of using the present value to estimate the worth of a sum of money received in the future can be extended to an arbitrary cashflow.

If there are a series of cash amounts that become available on different dates then the best way to gauge their value is to reduce each one to its present value and then sum them to form the Net Present Value.

That is if S_i is received at the end of time period *i* then the NPV is given by:

```
NPV = S₁/(1 +I )+S₂/(1 + I)^2+S₃/(1 + I)^3 ....Sₙ/(1 + I)^n
```

That is, the NPV is the total of all of the cash sums, each one discounted by the appropriate factor.

In more mathematical terms the NPV is:

$$NPV = \sum_{i=1}^{n} \frac{S_i}{(1+I)^i}$$

For example, if an investment promises to generate a cashflow of $100 at the end of the first year, $200 at the end of the second and $500 as a closing payment, then the Net Present Value is:

```
=100/(1+I)+200/(1+I)^2+500/(1+I)^3
```

where I is the effective annual rate of interest.

If I is assumed to be 8% then the NPV is $660.98 which should be compared to the total income of $800.

NPV function

Most spreadsheets have an NPV function which will calculate the present value of a cashflow:

```
=NPV(I,range)
```

where range is the part of the row or column that holds the cashflow values.

An alternative form is often provided:

```
=NPV(I,list of values)
```

where the values are entered directly into the formula.

The cashflows are assumed to arrive at the end of equal periods and the interest rate specified has to be appropriate for this period.

In the case of the cashflows described earlier, the following spreadsheet demonstrates the two methods of calculation - calculating the PV for each individual value and then adding the results up; and, more directly, using the NPV function.

	A	B	C	D
1	Interest	8%		
2			PV	
3	1	100	£92.59	
4	2	200	£171.47	
5	3	500	£396.92	
6	Total=	800		
7	NPV=		£660.98	£660.98
8				

The cashflows are entered into B3..B5 and the present values of amount is calculate in column C. The NPV in C7 is obtained by summing the present values listed above. That is, the formula in C3 is:

```
=PV($B$1,A3,,-B3)
```

which is copied down the column and summed in C7.

Alternatively the formula:

```
=NPV(B1,B3..B5)
```

entered into D7 calculates the NPV of all of the values in one step.

Irregular time periods

in most spreadsheets, the NPV function only works with equal intervals. It assumes that each cash sum specified is received at the end of a regular time period. If you want to calculate the PV of a cashflow at unequal intervals you can always use the basic formula on each payment, that is discount each sum and find the total.

For example, if you receive payments of:

1. $500 after 6 months
2. $1000 at the end of one year
3. $1500 at the end of the second year
4. $2000 at the end of the third year

The NPV can be calculated as shown:

	A	B	C
1	Interest=	6%	
2	Year	Cash flow	PV
3	0.5	£500.00	£485.64
4	1	£1,000.00	£943.40
5	2	£1,500.00	£1,334.99
6	3	£2,000.00	£1,679.24
7			£4,443.27
8			

An irregular cashflow

Notice the use of fractional years. The value entered in C3 to express 6 months is 0.5 of a year.

The present value of each cashflow is calculated in by entering:

```
=B3/(1+$B$1)^A3
```

in C3 and then copying this down the column. Notice that the discount formula uses the interest rate stored in B1, hence the use of an absolute cell reference.

Finally to get the NPV enter the formula:

```
=SUM(C3..C6)
```

into C7.

This first principles method can always be used to calculate the NPV. As long as you record the time that each sum is received using fractions if necessary then the NPV calculated will be correct.

An alternative to the direct approach is to reduce all of the payments to the smallest interval of time and use the NPV function. For example, in the cashflow used earlier the smallest interval is 6 months so we could record all of the cashflows in terms of a basic 6 month period.

Of course some of these cashflows would be zero but this doesn't alter the calculation of the NPV.

You can see the result of doing this below. You can see that the annual payments are simply the consequence of no payment half way through the year! The cashflow can now be reduced to its NPV using the NPV function in the usual way.

	A	B	C	
1	Interest=	6%		
2	Effective=	2.96%		
3	Half year	Cash flow	PV	
4	1	£500.00	£485.64	
5	2	£1,000.00	£943.40	
6	3	£0.00	£0.00	
7	4	£1,500.00	£1,334.99	
8	5	£0.00	£0.00	
9	6	£2,000.00	£1,679.24	
10			£4,443.27	
11				

Converting irregular to regular cashflow

The only question is, what interest rate is appropriate? You might think that as the rate is 6% per annum the appropriate rate for a half yearly cashflow is 6%/2. This isn't the case because it doesn't take into account the different compounding periods.

The correct interest rate to use is the effective interest rate calculated from the annual rate. As explained in Chapter 3, the effective rate gives you an interest rate that can be applied over a different compounding period while still giving the same result as the original rate. The formula relating the two is simply:

```
effective = (1 + I)^m-1
```

where m is the new compounding period measured in units of the original period. In this case m=.5 and the formula for the effective rate is:

```
(1+B1)^.5-1
```

which should be entered into B2. Now the NPV formula can be entered into B10:

```
=NPV(B2,B4..B9)
```

You can see that the result is the same as the first calculation. Whenever you alter the period of an NPV calculation you must make sure that the interest rate that you are using is the appropriate one. As the NPV calculation is based on compound interest, rates should be converted using the nominal to effective formula.

Net Future Value

In the same way that we can define the Net Present Value of an irregular cashflow we can define its Net Future Value. Each of the terms in the cashflow is multiplied by $(1+I)^{\wedge}m$ where m is the number of periods from the end of the loan that the payment is received. That is, if \$$S_i$ is received at the end of period i then:

```
NFV = S₁(1 + I)^n-1 + S₂(1 + I)^n-2 + S₃(1 + I)^n-3....Sₙ
```

You can see that the NFV is just the amount that you would accumulate if you invested each of the cash sums as soon as it was received at I% for the remainder of the term of the investment.

In more mathematical terms, the NFV is:

$$NFV = \sum_{i=1}^{n} S_n (1+I)^{\,n-i}$$

For example, if an investment promises to generate a cashflow of \$100 at the end of the first year, \$200 at the end of the second and \$500 as a closing payment then the Net Future Value is:

```
NFV = 100*(1 + I)^2 + 200*(1 + I)^1 + 500
```

where I is the effective annual rate of interest.

If I is assumed to be 8% then the NFV is \$832.64, which should be compared to the total income of \$800 and the NPV of \$660.98. You should be able to see from this example that the NFV really is just the amount you accumulate by investing each of the cashflows as they arrive.

The NPV NFV relationship

For each cash sum in the cashflow the NPV discounts it back to what would have to be invested to produce the sum and the NFV compounds it forward to what it would produce if invested immediately it is received.

There is a very simple and general relationship between NPV and NFV:

```
NFV = NPV*(1 + I)^n
```

In other words, if you invest the NPV for n years at I% the final sum is the NFV.

To see that this is true (skip this section if you are happy to take it all on trust) all we need to do is return to the general formula of the NPV and multiply it by $(1+I)^{\wedge}n$:

$$NFV = [\, \frac{S_1}{(1+I)} + \frac{S_2}{(1+I)^2} + \frac{S_3}{(1+I)^3} \cdots \frac{S_n}{(1+I)^n} \,](1+I)^n$$

If you multiply through by $(1 + I)^n$ you get:

$$NFV = \frac{S_1}{(1+I)}(1+I)^n + \frac{S_2}{(1+I)^2}(1+I)^n +$$

$$\frac{S_3}{(1+I)^3}(1+I)^{n...} \frac{S_n}{(1+I)^n}(1+I)^n$$

When you cancel the $(1+I)^i$ factor on the bottom of each term from the $(1+I)^n$ factor this gives:

$$NFV = S_1(1+I)^{n-1} + S_2(1+I)^{n-2} + S_3(1+I)^{n-3}...S_n$$

which is, of course, the definition of the NFV given earlier.

Hence the NFV really does always equal the NPV multiplied by $(1+I)^n$.

In more mathematical terms, what we have just shown can be written as:

$$NPV(1+I)^n = \sum_{i=1}^{n} \frac{S_n}{(1+I)^i}(1+I)^n$$

Canceling out the $(1+I)^i$ with the $(1+I)^n$ gives:

$$NPV(1+I)^n = \sum_{i=1}^{n} S_n(1+I)^{n-i}$$

You should once again recognize the right-hand side as being the definition of the NFV.

Because of this simple relationship there is no need for an NFV financial function. In all cases you can use

```
NFV = NPV(I,range)*(1 + I)^n
```

where n is the number of cashflows.

Notice that all of this still assumes that the cashflows occur at the end of each period. If this is not the case then slight modifications have to be made, but the general principles remain unchanged and the relationship between the two values still holds.

A regular cashflow

Now that we have a definition of both the NPV and NFV it it time to use them to look at some situations that we have already analyzed in earlier chapters. In particular, what is the NPV or NFV of a perfectly regular cashflow as might be found as part of a repayment loan, annuity or savings plan.

If you receive \$S at the end of each period for n periods the NPV is given by:

```
=S + S/(1 + I)+S/(1 + I)^2 + S/(1 + I)^3 ... S/( 1+ I)^(n-1)
```

which should remind you of the calculation to find the future value of a cashflow. In that case the sum was the same, but each value of S was multiplied by (1+I) raised to a power. By comparing the two expressions it isn't difficult to work out that:

$$NPV = S * \frac{1-(1+I)^{-n}}{I}$$

Comparing this to the formulas given in Chapter 4 also reveals that:

```
NPV = PV(I,n,S)
```

In other words, the NPV of a regular cashflow is just its present value as calculated in Chapter 4. This is very reasonable as the present value of a cashflow is simply what it would be fair to pay if you were purchasing an annuity. Put another way, it is the amount you need to invest now to generate the cashflow at I% per annum.

If you regard the cashflow as the repayments of a loan then the present value is equal to the amount of the loan. Again this is perfectly reasonable.

In the case of a savings plan the reasoning is slightly different because there is no sum of money changing hands now; only the cashflow is being invested. However, there is a well defined future value - the final value of the investment. In this case the present value is the amount that you would have to invest now to produce the same future value as the cashflow.

For example, if you invest \$1000 per annum at 10% (effective) for 10 years the future value is:

```
=FV(10%,10,-1000)=$15,937.42
```

and the present value is

```
=PV(10%,10,-1000)=$6144.567
```

If you invest \$6144.56 at 10% for 10 years you will receive:

```
=6144.57*(1+0.1)^10
```

which works out to \$15,937.42.

So investing $1000 per year for 10 years is the same as a making a one-off investment of approximately $6,144. Again the concept and terminology of 'present value' of a cashflow makes perfect sense.

You can choose to look at either the present value or the future value of a cashflow. In each case the future value is what the cashflow is finally worth and the present value is what it is worth now allowing for interest at I%.

No matter what the source or the purpose of the cashflow is the present value is calculated using:

$$PV = S * \frac{1 - (1+I)^{-n}}{I}$$

or the corresponding PV function and the future value is calculated using:

$$FV = S * \frac{(1+I)^{-n} - 1}{I}$$

or the corresponding FV function.

In each case the PV and FV are equal to the NPV and NFV and they are related by the standard formulas:

```
FV = PV*(1 + I)^n
```

and

```
NFV = NPV*(1 + I)^n
```

For simplicity we are assuming that all cashflows are at the end of each time period.

This idea of present and future values of a cashflow has a pleasing symmetry but the interpretation of PV and FV is different in each of the standard situations of a repayment loan, annuity and savings plan, as summarized in the following table, which assumes a series of equal cash payments.

Cashflow from	Present value	Future value
Loan	The amount of loan	The final value of the repayments if reinvested at I%. Equivalent to investing the amount of the loan at I%
Annuity	The amount that has to be invested to generate the cashflow i.e. the price of the annuity	The final value of the cashflow if reinvested at I %. Also equivalent to investing the price of the annuity at I%
Savings plan	The amount that has to be invested to give the same future value as the cashflow	The final value of the plan

You can see that in the case of a repayment loan and the annuity the present value is more meaningful than the future value and in the case of the savings plan both are meaningful.

Including all of the payments

There seems to be a contradiction contained in the previous section.

In Chapter Six we worked out the formula for a repayment loan based on the fact that its future value was zero and yet in the last section the idea that a repayment loan has a large positive future value was introduced.

The difference is that in the previous chapter we included the amount of the loan as the first amount in the cashflow. That is, the cashflow was assumed to start with a negative amount equal to the loan. If you include the initial negative amount in either the repayment loan or the annuity then we no longer have a simple regular cashflow.

Fortunately it isn't too difficult to arrive at similar results but they are different. Now that we have a general definition of the NFV and a relationship between the NPV and NFV we can re-examine the repayment loan and the annuity including their initial payments.

Notice that in both cases the first cashflow occurs right at the very start of the investment, that is at the start of the first period. This means that in the calculation of the NPV you simply include the first cash amount without the need to discount it. This is true of any sort of investment that involves an initial deposit which then generates a series of cashflows.

That is:

```
NPV of investment = -initial sum + PV of cashflow
```

If you include the amount of the loan or the purchase price of an annuity as the first item in the cashflow the NPV is zero. The reason is quite simply that the NPV of the cashflow is equal to the loan or purchase price as discussed earlier.

To see that this is so, let's look at an example.

If you borrow $1000 for 5 years at 10% (effective) per annum the repayments are $263.80 annually for 5 years.

Taking the cashflow as five yearly payments (at the end of each year) of $263.80, we can ask what the present value of this cashflow is:

```
PV = PV(10%,5,-263.80) = $1000
```

i.e. the amount of the loan.

If we now include the loan in the cashflow as an initial -1000 outflow of cash then the Net Present Value is -1000+1000, which is of course $0. This is also the result computed by the NPV function as long as you remember to include the initial sum separately.

If we include the initial amount of the loan as a negative sum then it is clear that the Net Future Value of a repayment loan is also zero.

Once again an example will make this clear.

If you borrow $1000 at 10% per annum to be repaid over 10 years then repayments are $162.75 per annum and the Net Future Value is:

```
-1000*(1+0.1)^10+FV(10%,10,-162.75)
```

which works out to zero.

You can arrive at the same conclusion by recalling the fact that the NFV is also given by the NPV invested at I% for the same period. Of course this implies that if the NPV is zero then then the NFV also has to be zero.

The same sort of reasoning applies to an annuity. If you include the initial deposit needed to fund the annuity then its present value and its future value are both zero. In the case of a savings plan there is no initial deposit and so the earlier interpretation of the present and future values hold.

What is important here is that we get different answers depending on whether or not we include all of the cash sums involved in a transaction.

It is perfectly reasonable to analyze the cashflow that results from a transaction like a repayment loan in isolation from the value of the loan.

It is also perfectly reasonable to analyze the cashflow including the loan, but not only are the results different but they have to be interpreted in different ways.

Key points

- The present value of a sum to be received in the future is just the amount you would have to invest now to equal it. Similarly the future value of a sum you have now is just the amount it will grow to by the action of compound interest.

- That is:
  $$FV = PV*(1 + I)\wedge n$$
  and
  $$PV = FV/(1 + I)\wedge n$$

- The present value is a good way of judging the worth of a sum that becomes available in the future because it measures its effective value in today's terms.

- Inflation alters the purchasing power of the present and future value but not their relative monetary value.

- Inflation increases the true interest rate to the quoted market rate.

- The net present value NPV is just the sum of the present values of each item in the cashflow.

- The net future value NFV is the sum of the future values of each term in the cashflow.

- The NPV and NFV are always related by the formula:
  $$NFV = NPV*(1 + I)\wedge n$$

- The NPV and NFV of a regular cashflow are identical to the PV and FV worked out in Chapter 4 in connection with the savings plan.

- In the case of the annuity and repayment loan the result that you get is different if you take the initial payment into account. In this case the cashflow isn't regular and the NPV and NFV are both zero.

Chapter 8

Investment Analysis

Now that we understand that Net Present Value provides a reasonable measure of worth, we can move on to explore how NPV can be used to make evaluate investments that generate irregular cashflows..

NPV and investments

Looking at the special case of the NPV of repayment loans, annuities and savings plans leads on to the consideration of more general investments. The idea of Net Present Value is perfectly applicable to cashflow and includes both positive and negative amounts over its entire lifetime.

The negative flows represent the cost of the investment and the positive flows indicate the return on the investment. As long as we include all of the cash sums involved, the NPV represents the value of the entire investment, i.e. the amount that would have to be invested at I% to produce the same worth as the whole cashflow.

Notice that the NPV is does not represent the amount of money that you put into the investment - that is represented by the negative cashflows.

We clearly need to investigate a little more closely what the NPV of the total cashflow of an investment actually means. The real question is what the negative quantities in the cashflow represent when reduced back to their present value.

If the cashflow has an entry of -5000 at the end of the 3rd year, say, then what this means is that you are investing $5000. An alternative way of making this cash deposit at the end of the 3rd year is to deposit $5000/(1+I)^3 now, that is $3756.57 assuming 10% per annum, and allow it to grow to the required sum.

In other words, the present value of a negative sum represents the amount you would need to invest now to produce the sum you need to invest in the future.

So in a cashflow containing both positive and negative values:

- the present value of each positive sum is the amount you would have to received now to produce the same sum in at the same point in the future
- the present value of each negative sum is the amount you would have to invest now to give the amount that you want to invest at the same point in the future

You can see that the NPV reduces both positive and negative cashflows to a fixed point in time, i.e. now and then adds them.

- If the total NPV is zero then this means that the amount that you invest is exactly equal to the amount that you receive back if you allow for the effect of the I% interest rate.
- If the total NPV is positive then you have received more than you invested and if negative you have made a loss on the investment.

This interpretation makes it very easy to formulate the basic rule of investment decision making.

If you are considering an investment that leads to a cashflow, then to decide if the investment is worthwhile compute its NPV and accept the investment if the NPV is positive.

If the NPV is zero then you should be indifferent to the investment, unless it has non-financial considerations that are not represented by the cashflow.

If the NPV is negative then you are making a loss on the investment and you need a very good non-financial reason for accepting it!

For example, you are offered the chance to make a loan to a business start up of $5000 with the conditions that at the end of the first year you would receive nothing, in the second you would be repaid $1000 and in each of the third, and fourth years you would be repaid $3000. Assuming a 'safe' interest rate of 8%, the NPV can be calculated with this spreadsheet:

	A	B	C
1	Year		
2	0	-5,000.00	
3	1	0.00	
4	2	1,000.00	
5	3	3,000.00	
6	4	3,000.00	
7	NPV	443.93	
8			

How good is the investment?

The cashflow is entered into B2:B6 and the formula in B7 is:

```
=NPV(8%,B3:B6)+B2
```

Notice that as the first payment is at that start of the first year it is entered as Year 0; this is a common convention concerning initial payments. The result of $443.93 indicates that there is a return over and above the 'safe' interest rate but how can we tell how good this return is?

A better investment?

If you are still not convinced about the importance of the NPV consider the result of making an alternative investment at the safe interest rate of I% using just the negative cashflows (recall that the negative cashflows are what you would have invested to receive the positive element of the cashflow). This represents what you could have earned on the money you have invested in the "risky" project if you had invested it into a "safe" project at the current safe interest rate. Of course if you had invested in the safe project then you wouldn't receive any of the positive values generated by the risky project - just the income from the investments at the safe interest rate.

Each such cash sum invested at I% will eventually grow to:

```
FV = -S₁*(1 + I)^m
```

where m is the number of time periods left to the end of the investment. The negative sign is needed simply because of our cashflow convention that an investment of $S represents a cashflow of -S.

This is simply the standard compound interest formula applied to each of the negative cashflows. The value of the entire "safe" investment is just the sum of all such values. It really is just the total you would receive from an alternative safe investment with the same cash outflows.

In other words, the future value of the safe investment FVsafe is just the sum of each negative cashflow compounded (at I%) forwards to the end of the investment.

Now the NFV of the original risky investment is the sum of the NFV of the negative and positive cashflow calculated separately so:

```
NFV(risk) = NFV(risk+) + NFV(risk-)
```

where NFV(risk+) is the NFV of the positive part of the cashflow and NFV(risk-) is the NFV of just the negative part of the cashflow. Again we assume that the interest rate used is the safe rate.

You can also see that the Future Value of the "safe" investment, i.e. the alternative where you simply invest your inputs, i.e. the negative cashflow items, at the safe rate is:

```
FV(safe) = -NFV(risk-)
```

that is, just the NFV of the negative components of the cashflow.

Putting these two together, we can see that the NFV of the original risky investment is just the NFV of the positive cashflows minus the NFV of the alternative safe investment. That is:

```
NFVrisk = NFV(risk+) - FVsafe
```

This gives us a basic relationship between the NFV of the entire cashflow and the NFV of the safe investment. Notice that this is what the entire risky investment is worth at the end of its term assuming that each item in the cashflow was invested at the safe rate.

Consider what this formula means if the NFV for the original 'risky' investment is zero. Then the NFV of the positive cashflow is equal to the total future value of the alternative safe investment.

That is, as:

```
NFVrisk = NFV(risk+)- Fvsafe = 0
```

we have:

```
NFV(risk+) = FVsafe
```

Thus you can see that when the NFV, and hence the NPV is zero, then the future value of the positive part of the cashflow is equal to the final value of the safe investment.

You do have to be very careful that you understand exactly what is being compared against what.

The safe investment involves depositing the negative cashflows at I% at the time that they would occur in the original investment. The future value of this investment is equal to the value of the positive cashflows in the original 'risky' investment but notice that for this to be true these also have to be invested as they are received at the 'safe' interest rate of I%.

Thus this comparison of values still takes into account the time when each sum of money is received. But as long as you do reinvest each sum of money at I% as it is received, NFV(risk+) really does represent the amount of money you have received at the end of the risky investment and of course FVsafe is the amount you receive at the end of the safe investment.

When these two quantities are equal the worth of both investments are is the same.

When the NFV and hence the NPV of the risky investment is positive:

```
NFV(risk+) > FVsafe
```

When it is negative then:

```
NFV(risk+) < FVsafe
```

In other words, a positive NPV does imply that you make more from the risky investment than from a safe investment at I% and a negative NPV indicates that you would be better off making the safe investment.

Borrowing at I% To Fund An Investment

Working out the NPV of an investment tells you how good it is compared to making a safe investment at I%.

You might be wondering if there is any relationship between making the safe investment at I% and borrowing the money to fund the risky investment at I %? You can see that this question is raised by the idea of using the market rate for capital as I% in the calculation of NPV.

The reasoning goes something along the lines of:

> *as the cash sums are discounted by the interest rate I% a positive NPV means that there is a profit to be made over and above the market rate.*

To make this more precise we need to work out exactly how borrowing the money needed for the investment affects the situation. If we assume that the cash sums received are used to pay off the loan then we can keep a current balance as each time period passes.

Suppose that the cashflow starts with a sum $\$S_1$ at the end of the first time period. This means that the at the end of the first time period the loan account stands at $\$S_1$. At the end of the second time period the cashflow received $\$S_2$ is added to the loan account along with the interest due to the debt:

`S₁*(1 + I) + S₂`

At the end of the third time period the loan account stands at:

`S₁*(1 + I)^2 + S₂^(1 + I) + S₃`

and so on.

You should recognize this as nothing more than the Net Future Value of the entire cashflow calculated using I%. In other words, the NFV is the profit that you would make on the investment if you borrowed the negative sums in the cashflow at I%. This gives us another interpretation of the NPV investment decision rule.

If the NPV is positive and you can borrow money at I% to make the investment then you will make a profit of NPV*(1+I)^n where n is the duration of the investment.

This interpretation takes our understanding of the NPV and its related NFV one step further and makes the NPV investment rule even more reasonable.

If an investment has a positive NPV, not only does it outperform a safe investment at an interest rate I%, it also gives a positive return even if the investment has to be funded by borrowing at I%.

NPV and NFV summary

We now have several good reasons for using the NPV as a measure of the 'goodness' of an investment.

A positive NPV calculated at I% implies that:

- the investment outperforms a compound interest investment based on the negative part of the cashflows at the same rate of interest.
- the investment is still profitable if the negative cashflows have to be borrowed at the same rate of interest.

In both cases it is assumed that it is possible to reinvest at I%. The NFV gives the profit made if the investment is funded by borrowing at I%.

Rate differentials

There is no doubt that at this point you may have noticed that there is an unrealistic assumption built into the calculation of the NFV. In calculating the interest paid on the loan and the interest earned on any positive deposits we have used the same rate of interest!

It is a well known fact that the rate for borrowing isn't the same as the rate for a saving. In most cases this difference can be ignored, but if you want a completely accurate answer then you really do need to calculate a 'modified' NFV using appropriate rates for the positive and negative sums.

If you do this in for the example earlier and assume that the rate for borrowing is 10% and that for a deposit is 8% then the appropriate calculation is

```
=NPV(8%,B3:B6)*(1 + 8%)^3 + B2*(1 + 10%)^4
```

The result is -$462.72.

In other words, if you take into account a 2% differential in interest rates for borrowing and saving then the investment that previously showed a profit now shows a loss.

Notice that in this case the NPV is unaffected by an interest rate differential because the negative sum is borrowed at the start of the investment - but this is not generally true.

Also notice that although the investment now makes a loss if the money has to be borrowed at 10% it still makes a better return than investing the same sum of money at 8%. In conclusion:

- If you have to borrow at more than I% to fund an investment, then a positive NPV isn't a guarantee that you will make a profit.

Chapter 9

Advanced Investment Analysis

While NPV (Net Present Value) is a very good and stable measure of the worth of an investment, there are many others. Perhaps the best known, and most complicated, is the Internal Rate of Return (IRR). Understanding exactly what it means is a good step toward making correct use of it.

Internal Rate of Return

IRR is the interest rate which reduces the NPV of the total cashflow to zero. In other words, it is the interest rate that you need to equal the investment. Clearly, if the NPV is zero then so is the NFV (Net Future Value).

Also notice that if the cashflows correspond to either a repayment loan or an annuity then the IRR is equal to the usual quoted interest rate.

Clearly the 'positive NPV' investment decision rule has a simple IRR equivalent:

- Accept any investment with an IRR greater than the prevailing interest rate.

Of course this raises the question of which the prevailing interest rate should be?

- If you are comparing the investment against the alternative of a safe investment then you should use the prevailing rate for deposits.
- If you are planning to borrow the money for the investment then the rate for loans should be used.

Also notice that the IRR calculation assumes that the money in the cashflow could be invested at the IRR rate, even though this rate my not be available on the open market. That is, if the IRR is 10% then this gives a zero NPV or NFV, assuming that any cash in the cashflow can be invested at 10%, which might well not be the case. This is considered to be a defect in the IRR as a measure of the worth of an investment – see the discussion of MIRR below for more information.

We are assuming that the value of money over time is governed by the computed IRR and not the prevailing safe market rates. So we need to find a value of I that results in the IRR rate that makes the NPV zero in this equation:

$$NPV = \sum_{i=1}^{n} \frac{S_i}{(1+I)^i}$$

It should come as no great surprise that the IRR cannot be calculated directly. To determine the IRR a complex equation involving all of the cashflows has to be solved. The only practical method of doing this is to use iteration. Fortunately, nearly all spreadsheets have an IRR function that lets you do this:

```
IRR(guess,range)
```

or

```
IRR(range,guess)
```

where the guess is an initial guess to start the iterative process and range is the part of the row or column that contains the cashflow data. Usually guess is an optional parameter.

A subtle point is that while the NPV function generally works with cashflows that occur at the end of each time period, the IRR function generally allows for the first cashflow to be at the start of the first time period. In other words, the IRR function assumes that the investment will be a conventional one with a cash outflow at the start and then positive or negative flows thereafter. For example, the cashflow below has the NPV and NFV as shown, assuming an 8% interest rate.

	A	B
1	Year	
2	0	(5,000.00)
3	1	0.00
4	2	1,000.00
5	3	3,000.00
6	4	3,000.00
7	NPV	443.93
8	NFV	603.96
9	IRR	10.87%
10		

Its IRR has been calculated in B9 using the formula

```
=IRR(B2..B6,10%)
```

As you can see, the IRR being over 8% suggests that the investment is worthwhile which is in line with the positive NPV. Notice the use of the guess of 10% as the initial value. If you really have no idea what the IRR is going to be or simply want to provide an automatic guess you could use

```
=IRR(range,RAND)
```

where RAND is a random number generating function.

Problems with the IRR

IRR is a very seductive measure of the worth of a cashflow because it looks so much like a simple interest rate that can be compared with other interest rates but it has a number of serious problems.

The first and most quoted of the defects in the IRR is the fact that it is possible for there to be more than one value that satisfies its definition.

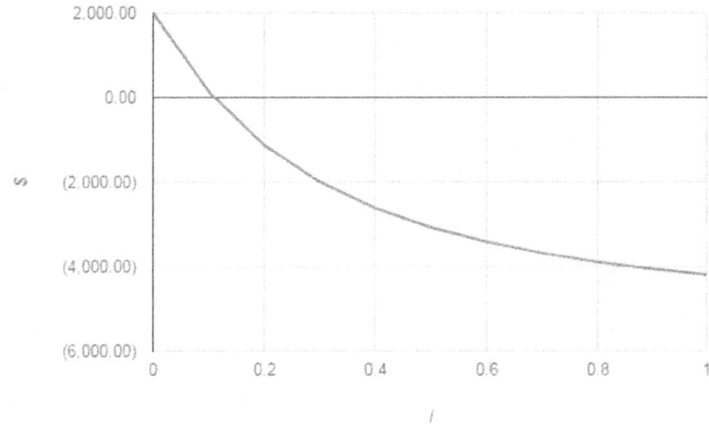

If you look at the graph of the NPV for a range of percentage rates then for the conventional investment cashflow the curve has the overall shape shown below.

You can see that the NPV falls as I increases. This is because the increase in the discount factor makes the positive cash sums worth less and less. Notice that the IRR is the value of I where the curve crosses the x axis, that is the value of I for which the NPV is zero.

If you draw the same graph for an unconventional type of investment, where the cashflow is at first positive and then negative, the result is a graph that increases with I.

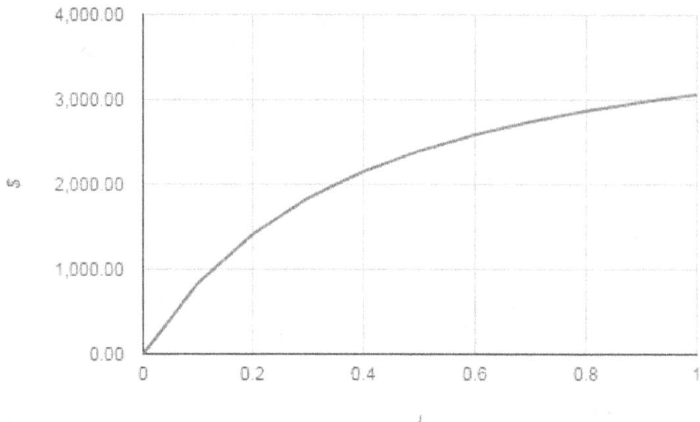

This curve is for the cashflow $4000 followed by -$1000 after each of four years. The reason that the NPV increases with I is that the negative sums are discounted more strongly as I increases and so the NPV actually increases.

In both of these cases there is a sensible value for the IRR because there is exactly one place where the graph cuts the x axis. However, it is possible to find cashflows which are a mixture of the conventional and the unconventional. This produces an NPV graph that has the characteristics of the two shown here.

Multiple solutions

Depending on the exact mixture of the two types of investment in the cashflow, the curve can be made to decrease and then increase, forming a U shape; or to increase and then decrease, forming an up-turned U.

For example the cashflow:

```
Year

0    -200
1     400
2     -50
3     -50
4    -400
```

produces the NPV shown in the following graph, Notice that in this case the cashflow has two possible values of IRR.

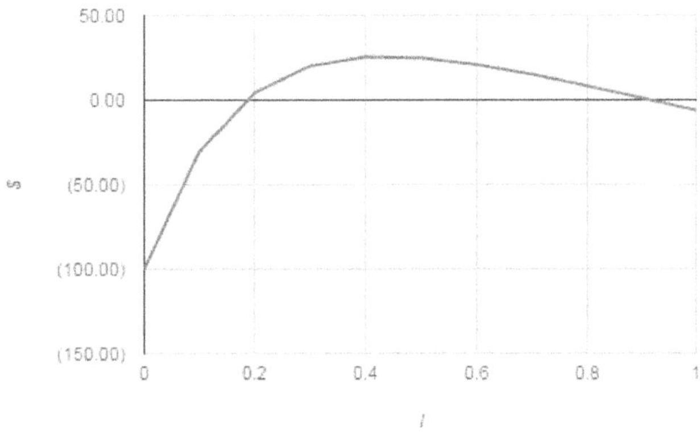

If you use the IRR function with this cashflow, which solution you find depends on the starting value you supply as a guess.

`IRR(range,10%)`

returns 18.37%, but

`IRR(range,80%)`

returns 91.35%.

Both are entirely valid IRRs and in a more general case there could be more than two such values. Indeed, there are even cases where no IRR exists at all because the NPV curve is always above the x axis, because the return on the investment is so good; or always below the x axis, because it is so bad. When you make use of the IRR function you have to keep in mind the possibility of multiple solutions and try a range of starting values to see if the solution changes.

Interpreting the IRR

The real problem, however, is not so much the existence of multiple IRR values, but how they should be interpreted. For example, if you apply the simple IRR investment decision making rule to the cashflow listed above with a market rate of 20% then, if you take the IRR to be 18.37%, you will reject the investment, but if you take it to be 91.35% you will accept the investment.

Which is correct?

The answer is that the use of this rule is too simplistic to cope with the realities of investment decision making. A true picture of what is happening can only be gained by examining the NPV versus I graph. From this you can quite clearly see that the investment is worth making for all values of I between 13.42% and 83.42%. because the NPV is positive in this range. However, you cannot conclude from this example that the range that lies between two values of IRR always corresponds to the acceptance range of interest rates. If you take the same cashflow and change the positive sums to negative and vice versa the result is an NPV curve that is the 'other way up' with respect to the original.

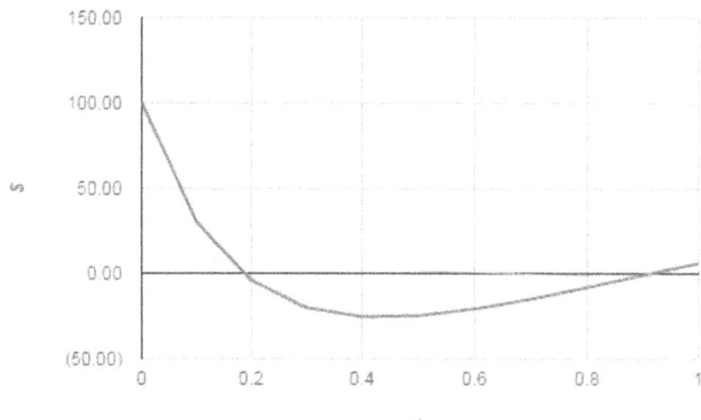

In this case the range of interest rates between the two IRR values produce a negative NPV and so for these rates the investment should be rejected. The acceptance region in this case corresponds to rates less than the lowest IRR and greater than the larger IRR value.

The NPV graph

Back in the days before the personal computer and spreadsheets there was a need for a simple measure of the 'goodness' of an investment. This led to the use of quantities such as the IRR as a simple index of profitability. However, as discussed, the IRR is flawed in that it simply marks the dividing line between positive and negative NPV values. In practice the region of positive NPV may correspond to a number of interest ranges. In this case there will be multiple values of the IRR, each one dividing an area of positive NPV from an area of negative NPV.

What is quite clear is that the IRR is an attempt to simplify a situation which, in many cases, cannot be so simplified. The best way of understanding the true nature of a cashflow is by viewing the NPV versus I graph. This tells you everything you could all need to know. All of the IRR values are clearly indicated and the regions of positive NPV.

Fortunately constructing such a graph is very easy with the aid of a spreadsheet, so much so that it should be a routine part of any investment analysis. Constructing a general spreadsheet that can cope with any cashflow isn't easy because of the need to allow for the variable duration of the investment. However it is quite easy to construct a spreadsheet that can deal with any cashflow up to a given maximum number of periods.

You can see an example spreadsheet here:

	A	B	C	D	E
1	Year	Cash Flow		I%	NPV
2	0	-5000		0	$9,700.00
3	1	1000		0.05	$5,630.66
4	2	1200		0.1	$2,899.49
5	3	-1000		0.15	$1,024.58
6	4	0		0.2	-$289.87
7	5	1000		0.25	-$1,229.76
8	6	2000		0.3	-$1,914.48
9	7	4000		0.35	-$2,422.22
10	8	4500		0.4	-$2,805.17
11	9	2000		0.45	-$3,098.72
12	10	0		0.5	-$3,327.31
13	11	0		0.55	-$3,508.00
14	12	0		0.6	-$3,652.92
15				0.65	-$3,770.79
16				0.7	-$3,867.94
17				0.75	-$3,949.04
18				0.8	-$4,017.56
19				0.85	-$4,076.13
20				0.9	-$4,126.73
21				0.95	-$4,170.88
22				1	-$4,209.77
23					

Column A and B contain the cashflow data. Notice that the year numbers are not actually used in the calculations and serve only to make entering the data easier. Column D is the range of percentages for which the NPV will be calculated. Tabulating the NPV for I ranging from 0% to 100% in 5% increments seems reasonable. Column E contains the NPV calculation.

Enter into E2:

`NPV(D2,$B$3..$B$14)+$B$2`

and copy this into E3..E22.

After this, entering a cashflow into column B results in the NPV for the full range of rates being calculated. Notice that if the cashflow stops before the 12th period then filling the remaining cells with 0 will not affect the NPV calculation.

Once you have the NPV table, all that remains is to define a graph that shows the data correctly. You should select an XY graph with I as the X data or data series 1 and NPV as Y or data series 2.

After suitable formatting, the result should look something like:

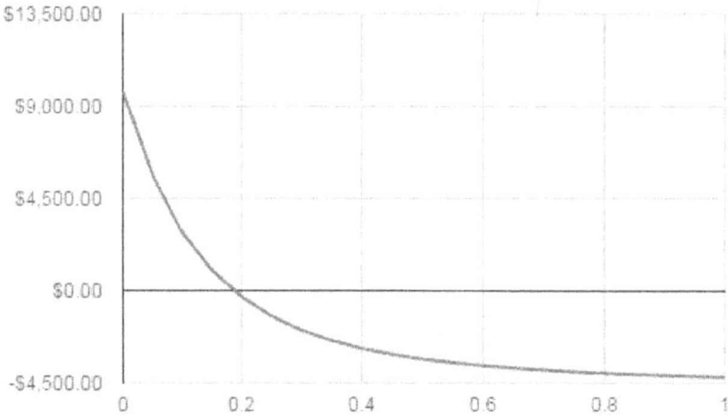

From this graph you can not only see that there is a single value of IRR of 19%, but you can also appreciate the sensitivity of the investment to changes in the assumed market rate.

Ranking investments

The positive NPV rule works very well if you are only interested in making a yes or no decision about an investment. What is more difficult is when there are a number of mutually exclusive investment opportunities and you have to choose just one to invest in. This investment choice problem requires potential investments to be ranked in order of 'quality'.

After our discussion of NPV and IRR these two quantities seem obvious candidates for ranking investment. However, they both need to be used with care and understanding. The main problem with the IRR is that it may not exist or may have multiple values. However when a single value does exist it still has a number of potential difficulties. The first is a characteristic shared by all percentage measures. If you have $10,000 and are offered two investments one at 9% and one at 10% it is immediately obvious which is the best. Most people would accept the 10% investment without a moment's thought.

However, if you are told that the two investments are mutually exclusive, i.e. you cannot accept both, but the 10% investment is limited to £100, you will begin to see that the situation isn't quite so simple.

In this case the maximum profit from the 10% investment is limited to £10 per annum but the 9% investment is limited only by the capital you have at your disposal and is potentially worth much more.

You might think that this either/or situation is contrived and in practice you would be able to invest the first £100 in the 10% yielding investment and the residual in the 9% investment. This is generally true when the investment is of a purely financial nature, but when other resources are involved then this mutually exclusive behavior is quite common.

For example, if the both investments make use of a limited resource - a machine, key personnel or management - then you may very well have to choose between a 10% and 9% return on a pair of mutually exclusive projects.

In general:

- If there is no limit on the amount that can be invested then it is reasonable to rank potential investments by a percentage measure of return.

- If there are limits on the amount invested in each case then percentage rankings can be misleading.

One way to think about this is realize that ranking investments by IRR would favor an investment of £1 that made a return of £2 over more reasonably sized investments that offer a lesser rate!

If it is the total amount of the return that matters, then mutually exclusive investments should be ranked by NPV. However, this is not to say that the 'efficiency' of the investment isn't of concern. It is quite common to work out the 'profitability index', PI, which is simply the NPV of the cashflow not including the initial investment divided by the initial investment. That is

```
PI = NPV(return cashflow)/investment
```

You should be able to see that the positive NPV rule is the same as accepting investments with a PI greater than 1. This is fine, but as the PI is a relative measure of profitability it shares the problem of being a percentage measure when it comes to ranking mutually exclusive alternatives. The PI index should be used as a measure of the efficiency of an investment but not as a way of choosing between mutually exclusive alternatives.

At this point you may think that the argument is all in favor of using the NPV as a way of ranking projects and this is in the main true. However, you need to be aware of the way that NPV can change with different rates of interest. It is quite possible for the NPV to give different rankings depending on the interest rate chosen.

For example, consider the two NPV curves shown below:

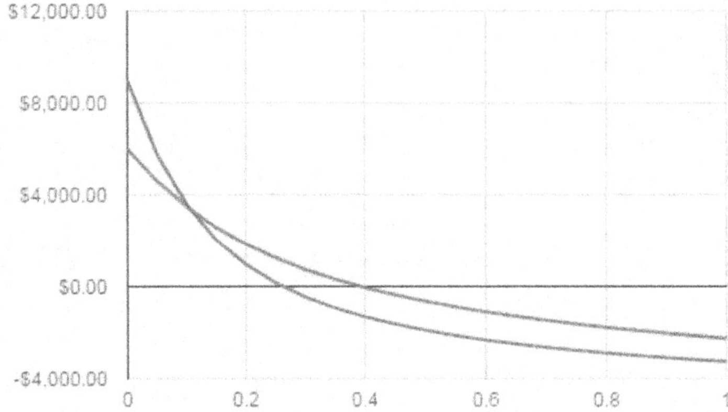

For values of interest lower than 10% Project 1 has a higher NPV than Project 2. However, for rates greater than 10% this ranking is reversed. This is a result of the of the former investment returning more money earlier than the other.

Also notice that the IRR, i.e. where the lines cross the $0 axis, ranks Project 2 much higher than Project 1, even though for moderate interest rates Project 1 has a much higher return than Project 2. This change in ranking isn't an artifact but a true reflection of the changing desirability of each investment as the interest rate for a safe investment changes.

Once again the NPV graph proves itself to be of more value than a simple index of worth.

Modified IRR - MIRR

There have been a number of attempts to find a percentage measure of an investment's worth that does not have the failings of the IRR. The most obvious modification to try to include is to apply different interest rates to the positive and negative cashflows.

One approach to doing this leads to the Modified Internal Rate of Return, which is often available to spreadsheet users as the MIRR financial function.

The key idea is that a reasonable definition of a rate of return is to compare the present value of all of the negative cashflows, i.e. the NPV, to the future value of the positive cashflows, i.e. the NFV. This reduces a complex investment to something that has just two events - an investment of the PV at the start and the receipt of the FV at the end.

The standard relationship between the NFV and NPV is just:

```
NFV=NPV*(1+I)n
```

where n is the total number of periods in the project.

Solving for I in this case gives the Modified Internal Rate Of Return, MIRR.

$$MIRR = \sqrt[n]{\frac{NFV}{NPV}} - 1$$

This all seems very reasonable and the MIRR has the advantage that it doesn't suffer from the IRR's tendency to have multiple values and it doesn't assume that all cashflows are subject to the IRR as interest rate for the life of the project. However, there are usually two interest rates that you do have to estimate. When you compute the NPV and the NFV you have to assume an interest rate for each.

If you read the MIRR literature and examine examples, you will encounter long discussions about how to set these rates. It is usually suggested that the positive sums in the cashflow should be discounted by a reinvestment rate and the negative sums of money in the cashflow should be discounted by a finance interest rate, i.e. the rate at which money would be borrowed. However, if you think about the operational definitions of NPV and NFV, it is clear that a good choice is to set both rates to the interest rate that money can earn from a safe source.

For example, if a project needs you to invest S_i in the future, i.e. at period i, you can invest:

```
PVᵢ = Sᵢ/(1 + finance)^i
```

now which will grow to Si at period i.

So the finance rate should be set to the rate that you can get on a PVi at the start of the project that gives you the amount you need to invest. In many cases this is the safe interest rate.

By the same reasoning, if the investment generates Si in the future this can be instantly reinvested at the reinvestment rate and this yields:

```
Fvᵢ = Sᵢ*(1 + reinvestment)^(n-i)
```

at the end of the investment.

Again, in many cases it is the safe investment rate that is appropriate.

The principle is clear:

- The finance rate should be the interest rate you can earn on a deposit when it isn't part of the project and the investment rate should be the interest rate you can earn on a deposit when it isn't part of the project.

Notice that the MIRR reduces the importance of cash inputs and cash outputs that are late in the project. That is, spending money later in a project is good because it has a lower present value and receiving money early is good because it is available to reinvest.

This description of how the MIRR is calculated can be summarized as:

1. Find the NPV of the negative part of the cashflow using the finance interest rate. This can be regarded as the present value of the total to be amount invested.

2. Find the NFV of the positive part of the cashflow using the reinvestment interest rate. This can be regarded as the future value of the total investment income.

3. Compute the MIRR using:

$$MIRR = \sqrt[n]{\frac{NFV}{NPV}} - 1$$

The MIRR isn't an easy calculation to do, but most spreadsheets have a special MIRR function:

```
=MIRR(cashflow range,finance rate,reinvestment rate)
```

For example, if you compute the IRR for the cashflow shown in the previous spreadsheet:

```
=IRR(B2:B14)
```

the IRR is 19% in agreement with the NPV diagram.

This makes the investment look very good against a 2% assumed safe rate.

If we assume the finance and the reinvestment rate is 2% the MIRR can be calculated using:

```
=MIRR(B2:B14,2%,2%)
```

which works out to 12% which is still better than the safe rate, but not quite as promising.

The MIRR is a controversial topic in finance and most people prefer the NPV or the IRR. However, the MIRR is very realistic in that it relates what you have to invest now to what you will receive at a point in the future. It reduces all cashflows to the start and end of the project and, as long as you understand the way that this works, you can set the finance and reinvestment interest rates to something that suits your situation.

Index